THE POGROMS
IN UKRAINE, 1918–19

The Pogroms
in Ukraine, 1918–19

Prelude to the Holocaust

By Nokhem Shtif,
translated and introduced
by Maurice Wolfthal

https://www.openbookpublishers.com

© 2019 Maurice Wolfthal. Preface © 2019 Grzegorz Rossoliński-Liebe.

ISBN Paperback: 978-1-78374-744-3
ISBN Hardback: 978-1-78374-745-0
ISBN Digital (PDF): 978-1-78374-746-7
ISBN Digital ebook (epub): 978-1-78374-747-4
ISBN Digital ebook (mobi): 978-1-78374-748-1
ISBN XML: 978-1-78374-749-8
DOI: 10.11647/OBP.0176

Cover image: Abraham Manievich, *Destruction of the Ghetto, Kiev* (1919). Jewish Museum, New York. Public Domain, https://thejewishmuseum.org/collection/3474-destruction-of-the-ghetto-kiev
Cover design: Anna Gatti.

Contents

Preface

Grzegorz Rossoliński-Liebe

It is as Bolsheviks that the Jews of South Russia have been massacred by the armies of [the Ukrainian leader Simon] Petliura, though the armies of Sokolov have massacred them as partisans of Petliura, the armies of Makhno as bourgeois capitalists, the armies of Gregoriev as Communists, and the armies of Denikin at once as Bolsheviks, capitalists, and Ukrainian nationalists. It is Aesop's old fable.

Israel Zangwill, *Jewish Chronicle*, 23 January 1920

The pogroms in Ukraine between 1917 and 1921 represent the largest and bloodiest anti-Jewish massacres prior to the Holocaust. The estimated number of Jews murdered in Ukraine in the aftermaths of World War I ranges from 50,000 to 200,000,[1] with many more Jews suffering violence, rape,[2] and loss of property. Altogether 1.6 million Jews were affected by these violent events. Although it is impossible to determine the exact number of victims of these pogroms, there is no doubt that this was the largest outbreak of anti-Jewish violence before the Shoah, the genocide during World War II in which 6 million European Jews, around two-thirds of the Jewish population of the continent, were systematically murdered by the Nazis and their collaborators.

---

[1]   The early pogrom researcher Nokhem Gergel estimated 50,000 to 60,000 victims. See Nokhem Gergel, "The Pogroms in the Ukraine in 1918–21," *Yivo Annual of Jewish Science* 6 (1951), 237–52 (p. 249).

[2]   On this topic see Irina Astashkevich, *Gendered Violence: Jewish Women in the Pogroms of 1917 to 1921* (Boston: Academic Studies Press, 2018), http://www.oapen.org/download?type=document&docid=1001750

   https://doi.org/10.11647/OBP.0176.01

Being overshadowed by the Holocaust, the pogroms in Ukraine are still not widely known. This unfortunate state of affairs is due to a number of factors. Firstly, the complex nature of the anti-Semitic violence perpetrated in 1917–1921 Ukraine. As hinted in Zangwill's quote above, the Jews were attacked by a number of different groups of perpetrators including Anton Denikin's Russian White Army, Simon Petliura's Army of the Ukrainian Republic, various peasant units, hoodlums, anarchists, and the Bolshevik Red Army.

These attacks stemmed from a number of grievances: accusations of supporting the enemy side, the chaos following the collapse of the old order, the aftermath of World War I and of the Russian Revolution, and a widespread anti-Semitism, after the dissolution of the Russian and Habsburg Empire. Furthermore, the perpetrators could easily locate their victims, as the areas affected were situated within the old Pale of Settlement, a region designated for Jews within today's Poland, Russia, Ukraine, Lithuania, Belarus, and Moldova.[3]

The relative lack of research on these events provides a further explanation of why the Ukrainian pogroms are much less known than the persecution the Jews suffered at the hand of the Nazis and other perpetrators during the Shoah. If, over the last 70 years, research on the Holocaust has resulted in several thousand publications, which can be housed only in the library of a large institute such as the United States Holocaust Memorial Museum, the publications relating to the pogroms of 1917–1921 would fill no more than two or three shelves. It is however hoped that the anti-Semitic campaigns taking place in early-twentieth-century Ukraine will in the future be recognized as an important chapter in the history of genocide studies.

Among the many perpetrators of the pogroms, it was Petliura who became the symbol of these massacres. Scholars have long debated whether Petliura was an anti-Semite who deliberately targeted the Jews, or a weak leader who could not stop their aggressors. Some answers

---

3   The Pale of Settlement was originally formed in 1791 by Russia's Catherine II. For political, economic, and religious reasons, very few Jews were allowed to live elsewhere. At the end of the nineteenth century, close to 95 percent of the 5.3 million Jews in the Russian Empire lived in the Pale of Settlement. In early 1917, the Pale of Settlement was abolished, permitting Jews to live where they wished in the former Russian Empire. This region continued to be a center of Jewish communal life until World War II. *YIVO Encyclopedia of Jews in Eastern Europe*, https://www. facinghistory.org/resource-library/image/pale-settlement

agent of Russian imperialism. [...] We have to and we will fight against the aspiration of Jewry to play the inappropriate role of lords in Ukraine. [...] No other government took as many Jews into its service as did the Bolsheviks, and one might expect that like Pilate the Russians will wash their hands and say to the oppressed nations, 'The Jew is guilty of everything'.[6]

Petliura continued to be glorified by nationalists well after his death. During the pogroms perpetrated by the Nazis and the Ukrainian nationalists in Lviv, the capital of western Ukraine, in the summer of 1941, the perpetrators staged the 'Petliura days' in his honor. After the main wave of pogroms in late June and early July 1941 came to an end, on 25 July 1941 the local nationalists organized with the Germans additional three days of pogroms to 'avenge' Petliura's assassination.[7] During the Cold War the Ukrainian diaspora celebrated him next to other national 'heroes' such as Stepan Bandera and Roman Shukhevych.

Moreover Ukrainian nationalist historians such as Taras Hunczak portrayed Petliura as a Judeophile who actively opposed the pogromists. Notwithstanding Petliura's responsibility for the pogroms, this revisionist approach is alive to this day — the one-time commander of the Army of the Ukrainian Republic is still hailed as a symbol of anti-Semitism and a 'national hero'. A monument to Petliura was unveiled in Vinnytsia in 2017.[8]

In contrast to Petliura, Anton Denikin did not become the symbol of the pogroms, although the massacres committed by his army were generally known. One important reason why he has not been associated with the anti-Semitic violence in Ukraine is his unspectacular life after the end of the Russian Civil War. When the Red Army defeated the White Army, he escaped with the rest of his soldiers to Crimea. In April 1920, he left to Constantinople and then to London. From 1926, he lived in France but he did not engage in politics, focusing on writing. The crimes committed by his army have not been forgotten but they were

---

6   Dmytro Dontsov, 'Symon Petliura', *Literaturno Naukoyi Vistnyk* 7–8:5 (1926), 326–28.

7   Grzegorz Rossoliński-Liebe, *Stepan Bandera: The Life and Afterlife of a Ukrainian Nationalist: Fascism, Genocide, and Cult* (Stuttgart: Ibidem, 2014). On the pogroms in Ukraine in general, see Kai Struve, *Deutsche Herrschaft, ukrainischer Nationalismus, antijüdische Gewalt: Der Sommer 1941 in der Westukraine* (Berlin: De Gruyter, 2015).

8   Taras Hunczak, 'A Reappraisal of Symon Petliura and Ukrainian–Jewish Relations, 1917–1921', *Jewish Social Studies* 31:3 (1969), 163–83.

to this complex question were put forward two decades ago by Henry Abramson, and more recently by Antony Polonsky and Christopher Gilley.[4] These scholars maintained that although Petliura's soldiers were responsible for the death of about forty percent of the victims, their commander's own behavior during the pogroms was ambivalent. On the one hand, Petliura seems not to have held anti-Semitic views and he did not personally issue orders to kill the Jews. On the other, he did very little to stop the massacres, particularly between January and April 1919, the period of the most brutal persecutions, even though the Ministry of Jewish Affairs urged him to do so. As Christopher Gilley writes, 'Petliura lacked the responsibility of agency for the pogroms, but as head of the army [he] must be held accountable for them.'[5]

Nevertheless, Petliura began to be seen as the main perpetrator of the pogroms only after his assassination on 25 May 1926 in Paris by Sholom Shwartzbard, a Russian-born French Yiddish poet of Jewish descent who had been in Ukraine during the massacres. The French court acquitted Schwartzbard, recognizing that he avenged the victims of Petliura's troops. This verdict enraged the Ukrainian nationalists who from now on claimed that Schwartzbard was a Bolshevik (or a Russian agent) who killed Petliura because he fought for an independent Ukraine. Interestingly Ukrainian nationalists had initially disliked Petliura due to his alliance with Józef Piłsudski in 1920. However, this view changed after his assassination, which, in their eyes, transformed Petliura into a hero who fought and died for an independent Ukraine. As Dmytro Dontsov, one of the leading radical Ukrainian nationalists, wrote after the trial:

> This murder is an act of revenge by an agent of Russian imperialism against a person who became a symbol of the national struggle against Russian oppression. It does not matter that in this case a Jew became an

---

4   Henry Abramson, *A Prayer for the Government: Ukrainians and Jews in Revolutionary Times, 1917–1920* (Cambridge, MA: Harvard University Ukrainian Research Institute and Center for Jewish Studies, 1999); Antony Polonsky, *The Jews in Poland and Russia, 1914–2008* (Oxford: The Littman Library of Jewish Civilization, 2010), III, 32–43; Christopher Gilley, 'Beyond Petliura: The Ukrainian National Movement and the 1919 Pogroms', *East European Jewish Affairs* 47.1 (2017), 45–61.

5   Gilley, 'Beyond Petliura', p. 47. See also Serhii Iekelchyk, 'Trahichna storinka Ukrains'koi revoliutsii: Symon Petliura ta Ievreis'ki pogrom v Ukraini (1917–1920)', in Vasyl Mykhal'chuk (ed.), *Symon Petliura ta ukrains'ka natsional'na revoliutsiia* (Kyiv: Rada, 1995), pp. 165–217.

neither investigated as thoroughly as the massacres done by the Petliura army nor did they arouse any major controversies, because none tried to systematically or deliberately deny them as the Ukrainian nationalists did in the case of Petliura's soldiers.

In order to understand the nature of the anti-Jewish violence between 1918 and 1921 in Ukraine, we need critical and nuanced studies instead of monuments and cults. A key source for further research into these massacres are the survivor accounts and early publications written by the survivors soon after the events. Nokhem Shtif's *The Pogroms in Ukraine: The Period of the Volunteer Army* is one such study. Shtif's book can be compared to the works published by the members of the Jewish Historical Commission, which was created in 1944 by survivors of the Shoah in liberated Poland. This group of young Jews collected several thousand survivor testimonies and published important early studies on the Holocaust.[9]

Shtif, a linguist, writer and journalist, was the editor-in-chief of the Editorial Committee for the Collection and Publication of Documents on the Ukrainian Pogroms, which was founded in Kiev in May 1919. He collected the material during the pogroms and published his book in Berlin in 1923. His study stands alongside Nokhem Gergel's *The Pogroms in Ukraine in the Years 1918–1921* and Elias Tcherikover's *Antisemitism and the Pogroms in Ukraine: The Period of the Central Rada and the Hetman, 1917–1918*, one of the most important early publications on the topic.[10] Unlike other authors, Shtif did not focus on Petliura and his troops but on Denikin's White Army. A particularly perceptive study of the violence inflicted on the Ukrainian Jews and its perpetrators, *The Pogroms in Ukraine, 1918–19: Prelude to the Holocaust* fills the gaps in our understanding of the largest massacres before the Holocaust. This translation from the Yiddish published in Open Access finally makes this important study accessible to scholars, students and the wider readership.

9   Laura Jockusch, *Collect and Record!: Jewish Holocaust Documentation in Early Postwar Europe* (Oxford: Oxford University Press, 2012).

10   Nokhem Gergel, 'The Pogroms in Ukraine in the Years 1918–1921', in *Shriftn far ekonomik un statistic*, I, 1928, English translation in *YIVO Annual of Jewish Social Science* (New York: Yivo Institute for Jewish Research, 1951), pp. 237–52; Elias Tcherikower, *Antisemitizm un pogromen in Ukraine, 1917–1918: tsu der geshikhte fun Ukrainish-Yidishe batsihungen* (Berlin: Mizreh-Yidishn historishn arkhiv, 1923).

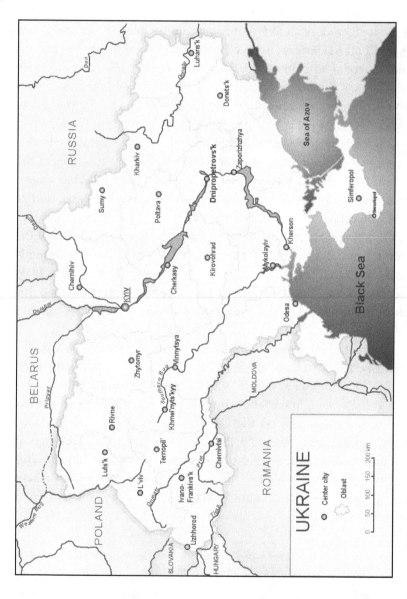

Political map of Ukraine by Sven Teschke. Wikimedia, https://commons.wikimedia.org/wiki/File:Map_of_Ukraine_political_enwiki.png

Introduction

Maurice Wolfthal

The signing of the armistice formally ending World War I did not end the bloodbath in Ukraine, which continued to be ravaged by the Civil War between the Soviet regime and the 'Whites', by Polish attempts to seize the former Austrian province of Galicia, and by Ukraine's campaign to maintain its independence from both Poland and the USSR. Organized armies, partisan units, and peasant gangs — with political objectives that were at times opposing and at times overlapping — devastated the land. As is often the case, unarmed civilians bore the brunt of the suffering. These military forces — the Ukrainian National Army headed by Symon Vasylyovych Petliura,[1] the Tsarist Volunteer Army[2] of Anton Ivanovich Denikin,[3] the Army of the Second Polish Republic, the gangs of such leaders as Nestor Makhno[4] and Nikifor Grigoriev,[5] and the Bolshevik Army — were guilty of specifically targeting Jewish communities.

---

[1]   Symon Petliura: Supreme Commander of the Army of the Ukrainian National Republic that was established in 1917, and head of the Directorate formed in 1918.

[2]   The *Dobrovolcheskaya Armiya* was organized in late 1917 by Gen. Mikhail Alekseyev and Gen. Lavr Kornilov to oppose the Bolsheviks.

[3]   Anton Denikin: A general in the Russian White Army fighting the Bolsheviks in the Russian Civil War, who took command of the Volunteer Army in April 1918, fighting mostly in Ukraine.

[4]   Nestor Makhno: Leader of anarchist revolutionary groups sometimes allied with the Red Army, sometimes with the Whites.

[5]   Nikifor Grigoriev: Nickname of Nychipir Servetmik, self-styled *ataman*, who first served in the Russian army, then led military groups allied variously with Petliura, Makhno, and others.

    https://doi.org/10.11647/OBP.0176.02

Scholarly estimates of the number of Jews killed, wounded, or tortured range between 100,000 and 120,000. William Henry Chamberlin[6] cites Sergei Gusev-Orenburgsky, who calculated that 'no fewer than 100,000 people perished.'[7] Hundreds of Jewish communities were burned to the ground. Zvi Y. Gitelman estimates that more than 1,200 pogroms were committed in Ukraine in 1918 and 1919.[8] The homeless numbered in the hundreds of thousands, including thousands of orphans living on the streets, rummaging for food, begging and stealing.

Working from large documentation that had been collected in Kiev and brought to Berlin, Nokhem Gergel published 'Di pogromen in Ukrayne in di yorn 1918–1921' in 1928,[9] in which he conservatively estimated the total number of murdered and maimed in those three years at 100,000. He also reported the horrific mass rapes of Jewish women and girls during these pogroms in Ukraine, noting several thousand documented cases, but indicating that there were probably many more, because 'The victims took pains to conceal their disgrace.'[10]

A number of local and international relief organizations struggled to provide the pogrom survivors with food, lodging, and medical care. The situation was desperate not only for those who had been maimed, blinded, or raped, but also those who were falling prey to deadly epidemics. In the course of their work, some of the Jewish agencies attempted to document the atrocities to encourage donations for their relief work and to mobilize world public opinion against the pogroms. To that end, they contacted news agencies and diplomats, especially those of the Western powers that were supporting the 'White' anti-Bolshevik armies with funding and weapons.

In what was one of the earliest efforts to systematically record human rights atrocities on a mass scale, the Central Committee for the Assistance of Pogrom Victims in Kiev combined the efforts of three relief agencies into a single *Redaktions-kolegye oyf zamlen un oysforshn di materialn vegn*

---

6   William Henry Chamberlin, *The Russian Revolution 1917–1921* (New York: Macmillan, 1954), II, p. 240.

7   *Kniga o evreiskikh pogromakh na Ukraine v 1919 g.* (Petrograd: Ispolneno izd-vom Z.I. Grzhebina, 192–?), p. 14.

8   Zvi Y. Gitelman, *Jewish Nationality and Soviet Politics* (Princeton: Princeton University Press, 1972), p. 161.

9   Nokhem Gergel, 'The Pogroms in Ukraine in the Years 1918–1921', in *Shriftn far ekonomik un statistic*, I, 1928, English translation in *YIVO Annual of Jewish Social Science* (New York: Yivo Institute for Jewish Research, 1951), pp. 237–52.

10   Ibid., p. 252.

di pogromen in Ukrayne,[11] composed of prominent Ukrainian Jews, with the scholars Nokhem Shtif and Elias (Elye) Tcherikover at the helm. The Editorial Board also added documentation that had been collected by other organizations, like the All-Ukrainian Relief Committee for the Victims of Pogroms under the auspices of the Red Cross.

But in 1920 and 1921 the Bolsheviks in Kiev began to suppress other political parties, including the Yidishe folks-partey[12] and its publishing house, the Folks-farlag.[13] This impelled Dubnow, a founder of the party, Shtif, Tcherikover, and other folkists who had compiled the archive to leave Kiev. They eventually made their way to Berlin, by way of Kaunas, Minsk, or Moscow, and brought the documents with them.

This was now known in English as the Eastern Jewish Historical Archive, in German as the *Ostjüdisches Historisches Archiv,* and in Yiddish as the *Mizrekh-yidisher historisher arkhiv.* The documentation was so large that a multi-volume series was planned for publication. The Board itself published only two volumes. Tcherikover's 1923 *Antisemitism and the Pogroms in Ukraine: The Period of the Central Rada and the Hetman, 1917–1918* came out in Yiddish and Russian.[14] Joseph B. Schechtman's *The Pogroms of the Volunteer Army in Ukraine* appeared later, in Russian and German,[15] in 1932. A second book by Tcherikover was only published in 1965. Nokhem Shtif researched the archive materials to write *The Pogroms in Ukraine: The Period of the Volunteer Army* in 1920, and published it in 1923 in Berlin with Verlag Wostok, in Yiddish and Russian. Tcherikover and Shtif deliberately published their works in Yiddish both to reach a Yiddish-reading audience and to signal the arrival of Yiddish as a serious academic language.

The archive received worldwide attention in a sensational trial a few years later. Sholem-Shmuel Schwarzbard was a young Jewish watchmaker from Balta who survived the 1905 pogrom. Drawn to

---

11 Yiddish: Editorial Board for the Collection and Investigation of Materials Concerning Pogroms in Ukraine.

12 Yiddish: Jewish People's Party, founded in 1906 by the historian Simon Dubnow and Yisroel Efroykin, was dedicated to the achievement of full civil and political rights for the Jews of the Russian empire. Its supporters saw it as a more realistic response to European anti-Semitism than the possibility of a Jewish state in Palestine.

13 Yiddish: People's Publisher.

14 Elias Tcherikover, *Antisemitizm un pogromen in Ukraine, 1917–1918* (Berlin: Yidisher literarisher ferlag, 1923).

15 Joseph B. Schechtman, *Pogromy Dobrovolcheskoi Armii na Ukraine* (Berlin: Ostjüdisches Historisches Archiv, 1932).

radical politics, he served time in prison due to his activities. He left Ukraine for the neighboring provinces of Austria-Hungary, where he worked as a watchmaker but continued to move in Socialist and Anarchist circles. He was arrested in Vienna and Budapest for robbery, left for Switzerland and then moved to Paris. Schwarzbard enlisted with his brother in the French Foreign Legion, then fought in the French Army in World War I. He was shot through the lung and was left with only one good arm, and was decorated for heroism with the Croix de Guerre. After his discharge he traveled back to Russia, where he joined a unit of Red Guards in Petrograd, then an Anarchist unit in Odessa. In 1919, when Schwarzbard saw the atrocities being perpetrated in pogroms by the 'Whites', he enlisted in an 'International Brigade' to fight against the forces of Petliura and Denikin. But his unit was routed, and he eventually managed to make his way back to Paris.

In 1926 Schwarzbard learned that Petliura, now the head of the Ukrainian government in exile, was living in Paris. He followed him and assassinated him. Arrested and charged with murder, Schwarzbard took full responsibility for killing Petliura to avenge the thousands of pogrom victims. There was a long, tumultuous trial, and Tcherikover, who was now Director of the History Section of the YIVO,[16] testified for the defense,[17] marshaling the harrowing atrocities that the Editorial Board had documented. The names were read aloud of fourteen of Schwarzbard's family members who had been murdered in the pogroms. Schwarzbard was acquitted.

Shtif's book *The Pogroms in Ukraine: the Period of the Volunteer Army* illuminates the Schwarzbard trial. Petliura's supporters made much of the fact that Schwarzbard was Jewish and had served in the Bolshevik Army. Shtif concludes that the primary cause of the Denikin pogroms was the anti-Semitism of the Volunteer Army officers, all of whom were Tsarists. He notes that during World War I, the Tsarist regime had already falsely accused the Jews of espionage and of betraying Russia to the Germans. Hundreds of thousands of Jews had been deported into the Russian interior on suspicion of treason, far from their villages and

---

16   Yiddish acronym for *Yidisher visenshaftlekher institut* [Jewish Scientific Institute], founded in 1925. Its prime mover had been Nokhem Shtif. It is now in New York, known as the Institute for Jewish Research.

17   Simon Dubnow also attended the trial.

towns near the front lines. Even earlier, Russians loyal to the monarchy had alleged that Jews were conspiring to bring the Bolsheviks to power. On top of the vicious stereotype of Jews as rich and greedy, there was now the canard that Jews were Communists. A common refrain was 'Kill the Jews and save Russia!'

Shtif pinpoints the anti-Semitic vitriol of the two ideologues of the Volunteer Army, Vasiliy Vitalyevich Shulgin and Konstantin Nikolayevich Sokolov. Shulgin had been a member of the last Russian *Duma* and a leader of the Black Hundreds,[18] and was editor-in-chief of the anti-Semitic newspaper, *Kievlyanin*. Sokolov had helped write the Constitution of the Volunteer Army and was head of Denikin's propaganda department, *Osvag*.[19] Both of them promoted paranoid delusions about an imaginary Judeo-Bolshevik conspiracy. In the 1920s and 1930s those same delusions were to permeate Nazi pathology and helped pave the way to the Holocaust. They continued to fuel pogroms even after the end of World War II, and they persist in some quarters today.

Shtif had been named on the Editorial Board because he was a leading Jewish intellectual and activist. Raised in a Yiddish-speaking home, he had received a traditional religious education from private tutors, and then attended the *Real-Gymnazium* as a teenager in Rovno. He immersed himself in the study of Hebrew. He later studied engineering and chemistry at the Kiev *Polytekhnikum* and became active in Socialist and Zionist causes. In 1902 he attended the Zionist conference in Minsk.

The bloody pogrom at Kishinev in 1903 prompted Shtif to join a Jewish self-defense unit in Kiev. He helped start the *Vozrozhdenie*[20] movement, which later evolved into the *Sejimist* Party.[21] He was jailed for his political activities and went into exile in Switzerland, where he was influenced by the thinking of Chaim Zhitlowsky, Yiddishist, advocate of Jewish Territorialism, and founder of the Socialist Revolutionary Party. Shtif began to contribute numerous articles and literary reviews

---

18   Russian: *Chornaya sotnya*. A violent ultranationalist, tsarist organization that called for the expulsion of Jews from Russia and for the suppression of Ukrainian political and cultural rights.

19   Russian acronym for *Osvedomitel'noe-agitatsionnoe otdelenie* [Propaganda and Information Department].

20   Russian: Renaissance.

21   Also known as the Jewish Socialist Labor Party.

to *Yevreyskaya Zhizn*,[22] *Dos naye lebn*,[23] *Di folksshtime*,[24] *Der fraynd*,[25] and other newspapers.

When Shtif returned to Russia he engaged in political work in several cities. He also volunteered at the *Khevra Mefitsei Haskalah*,[26] which fueled his academic interest in the field of Yiddish language and literature, and moved him further towards Yiddishism. He worked at the Jewish Colonization Association[27] and was an editor for the Vilna publisher, B. A. Kletzkin. Shtif attended the Law Lyceum in Yaroslavl and received a law degree in 1914. During World War I he worked at the *Evreiskii Komitet Pomoschchi Zhertam Voiny*.[28] After the revolution of 1917 he campaigned to revive the *Yidishe folks-partey*.

Shtif's first major scholarly work appeared in 1913 in the pioneering academic volume, *Der pinkes: Yorbukh far der geshikhte fun der yidisher literatur un shprakh, far folklor, kritik, un bibliografye*,[29] published in St. Petersburg, in which he wrote[30] a scathing review of Meyer Pines's *History of Jewish Literature*, which had been written in French as a Ph.D. dissertation at the Sorbonne and then translated into Yiddish. Dozens of reviews, articles, and essays were to follow in the next twenty years on literary history and criticism: Yiddish grammar, spelling, phonetics, linguistics, Socialism, and the Yiddishist movement.

After the Russian Revolution Shtif moved to Kiev and worked in journalism and politics. The Central Rada of the Ukraine People's Republic proclaimed Yiddish as one of its official languages, to be used in official documents and on national currency. It established a Ministry of Jewish Affairs, in addition to those for Polish and Russian affairs. It officially recognized a kind of 'Jewish autonomy'. Jews served in a variety of government positions. In 1919 Shtif developed

---

22 Russian: Jewish Life.

23 Yiddish: The New Life.

24 Yiddish: The People's Voice.

25 Yiddish: The Friend.

26 Hebrew: The Society for the Promotion of the Jewish Enlightenment.

27 Founded in 1891 by Baron Maurice de Hirsch to help Russian Jews leave Russia after the pogroms of the 1880s. It bought agricultural land in North and South America and set up communities of Russian Jews as farmers on those lands.

28 Russian: Jewish Committee in Aid of War Victims.

29 Yiddish: Annals: Yearbook for the History of Jewish Literature and Language, Folklore, Criticism, and Bibliography.

30 Under the pseudonym *bal-dimyen* [Master of the imagination].

many of his ideas in *Yidn un yidish, oder ver zaynen 'yidishistn' un vos viln zey?*[31]

Shtif immersed himself in the medieval Yiddish holdings of the Asiatic Museum in St. Petersburg and the archives in Kiev. Years later in Berlin he would study early Jewish manuscripts from Germany, Italy, and England. He contributed to the journal *Yidishe filologye*[32] and later edited *Di eltere yidishe literatur: literarishe khrestomatye, mit an araynfir un derklerungen tsu yeden shrayber.*[33]

Passionately committed to Jewish civil and cultural rights in Europe, and to the future of Yiddish — the vernacular[34] for nearly 11,000,000 Jews — Shtif disseminated an influential memoir, *Vegn a yidishn akademishn institut,*[35] in which he advocated the founding of a university-level institution whose courses and research publications would be in Yiddish, and whose focus would be the full range of Ashkenazic Jewish culture. Leading Jewish intellectuals discussed the possibilities, and the YIVO was founded in Berlin, but almost immediately moved to Vilna in 1925.

Shtif's lifelong devotion to Jewish affairs had moved him to take time and effort away from his academic interests; he worked with pogrom victims in Kiev, helped lead the Editorial Board, moved to Berlin with the others on the Board, and wrote *Pogromen in Ukrayne: di tsayt fun der frayviliger armey.*

Shtif does not aim to catalogue all the horrors of the Denikin pogroms. He attempts, rather, to discern their common pattern and to determine their military, historical, and ideological roots. He points out that the Volunteer Army was badly fed and equipped, and it relied on constant plunder for upkeep. He maintains that since most of Denikin's officers were Tsarist officers whose anti-Semitism was endemic, they either encouraged violence against Jews or tolerated it. He notes that during the

---

31 *Yidn un yidish, oder ver zaynen 'yidishistn' un vos viln zey?* (Kiev: Onheyb, 1919; Warsaw: Nayer ferlag, 1920).
32 Yiddish: Yiddish Philology.
33 Yiddish: *Old Yiddish Literature: a literary chrestomathy with an introduction and explanation for each author* (Kiev: Kultur-lige, 1929).
34 The Czernowitz Conference of 1908 had declared Yiddish to be 'a national language of the Jewish people.'
35 Yiddish: On a Jewish Academic Institute. First circulated as a memorandum, later published in *Di organizatsye fun der yiddisher visnshaft* (Vilna: Tsentraler Bilding Komitet, 1925).

war years immediately preceding the pogroms, the Tsarist regime had already falsely accused Russian Jews of espionage, of betraying Russia to the Germans, and of conspiring to bring the Bolsheviks to power. The old regime had severely curtailed their civil rights and had effectively wiped out dozens of Jewish communities by deporting hundreds of thousands of Jews far from their homes near the front lines on suspicion of treason. Furthermore, the regime had secretly supported the brutal, anti-Semitic Black Hundreds.

Shtif is at his most 'academic' when he brings to bear the tools of textual analysis on the writings of two prominent ideologues of the Volunteer Army, Vasiliy Vitalyevich Shulgin and Konstantin Nikolayevich Sokolov. Shulgin had been a Tsarist member of the last Russian *Duma* and was a close advisor to General Denikin. He was editor-in-chief of the anti-Semitic Kiev newspaper, *Kievlyanin*. Sokolov had been a jurist and law professor who had helped write the Constitution of the Volunteer Army. In 1919, when Sokolov was named by Denikin to head the Army's propaganda department, *Osvag*, he immediately fired all its Jewish workers.

Indeed, hatred of the Jews pervaded the top ranks of the Army. Peter Kenez has described this obsession with the myth of 'Judeo-Bolshevism' this way: 'Reading secret reports which were obviously not meant as propaganda, it is clear that this anti-Semitism, full of paranoid delusions, bordered on the pathological.'[36] In the 1920s and 1930s those same delusions of a Jewish-Bolshevik conspiracy permeated Nazi pathology and helped pave the way for the Holocaust. They continued to fuel pogroms even after the end of World War II.

Though Shtif enjoyed immense esteem as a scholar and a founder of the YIVO, he did not feel financially secure. In 1926 he and a few other Yiddishist academics returned to Ukraine, attracted by the Soviet Union's official ideology of respect for all its nationalities, by the funding of Yiddish scholarship, newspapers, literature, and theater, and by the promise of a decent salary. The following year he was named head of the Department for Jewish Proletarian Culture at the Ukrainian Academy of Sciences in Kiev, and he founded and edited its official journal, *Di yidishe shprakh*.[37]

---

36   Peter Kenez, *Civil War in South Russia, 1919–1920* (Berkeley: University of California Press, 1977), p. 172.
37   Yiddish: The Yiddish Language.

One of the aims of YIVO's founders was the systematization of Yiddish orthography, and great efforts had been made towards that end. The Soviet government, through its Jewish institutes, promoted the phonetic spelling of Yiddish words of Hebrew/Aramaic origin, which made reading easier and furthered its ideological aim to disguise those origins, which were denounced as being 'nationalistic,' 'bourgeois,' 'religious,' and 'Zionist.' Nokhem Shtif and his journal embraced Soviet Yiddish orthography.

The stage was being set for Stalin's Great Purge. Tens of thousands of Soviets were falsely accused of treason, espionage, 'Trotskyism,' 'rightist deviation,' etc. Many were coerced into 'confessing' their crimes. Thousands were fired from their jobs, expelled from the Communist Party, imprisoned, deported to undertake slave labor, or murdered outright. The Jewish victims were primarily rabbis, Zionists, Bundists,[38] and other non-Communist intelligentsia.

Shtif was suspect. He had belonged to a Zionist organization in his youth. He had maintained contact with the YIVO in capitalist Poland, many of whose leaders were anti-Soviet Bundists, and he had been an activist for the now-banned *Yidishe folks-partey*. He was soon demoted. His department was replaced by the new and much larger Institute for Jewish Proletarian Culture, with Yoysef Liberberg — a member of the Communist Party — named as its head, though Shtif continued to lead its Philological Section. In 1928 both he and Liberberg were publicly reprimanded by the Party for inviting the eminent historian Simon Dubnow to attend the opening of the Institute.

In 1929 Shtif went even further than the campaign for Soviet Yiddish orthography by publishing in his journal *Di sotsyale diferentsiatsye in yidish: di hebreyishe elementn in der shprakh,*[39] in which he derided the Hebrew/Aramaic component of Yiddish as a useless reactionary relic of the religious and upper classes. In 1931 Max Weinreich, one of the founders of the YIVO, and an equally eminent philologist, wrote a blistering rebuttal to Shtif in 1931, *Vos volt yidish geven on hebreyish?*[40] in

---

38   Members of the Algemeyner yidisher arbeter bund in lite, poyln, un rusland [The General Union of Jewish Workers in Lithuania, Poland, and Russia], founded in 1897.

39   Yiddish: *Social Differentiation in Yiddish: The Hebrew Elements of the Language.*

40   Yiddish: What Would Yiddish Be Without Hebrew?

the journal *Di tsukunft*[41] of New York. Shtif defended his position with *Revolutsye un reaktsye in der shprakh*[42] in his journal (now re-named *Afn shprakhfront*[43]) in 1931 and 1932.

But Shtif died in his office in Kiev the following year at the age of 54, and Weinreich wrote a generous obituary in *Di tsukunft*, praising Shtif's scholarly contributions and passionate idealism. As for their recent public clash of ideas, Weinreich made only passing reference to Shtif's articles, asking rhetorically whether they had really been the result of Shtif's own thinking or of some sudden political pressure.

---

41   Yiddish: The Future.
42   Yiddish: Revolution and Reaction in Language.
43   Yiddish: On the Language Front.

Further Reading

Astashkevich, Irina. *Gendered Violence: Jewish Women in the Pogroms of 1917 to 1921* (Boston: Academic Studies Press, 2018), http://www.oapen.org/downlo ad?type=document&docid=1001750

Abramson, Henry. *A Prayer for the Government: Ukrainians and Jews in Revolutionary Times, 1917–1920* (Cambridge, MA: Harvard University Ukrainian Research Institute and Center for Jewish Studies, 1999).

Bemporad, Elissa, with Efim Melamed, Jeffrey Veidlinger, and Eric Weitzy. 'A Forgotten Genocide: The Pogroms in Ukraine, 1918–1919, and their Impact on Memory and Politics', Video of discussion co-presented by the Center for Jewish History, https://www.youtube.com/watch?v=RlfQrgziSTk

Chamberlin, William Henry. *The Russian Revolution 1917–1921* (New York: Macmillan, 1954).

Dekel-Chen, Jonathan L. *Anti-Jewish Violence: Rethinking the Pogrom in East European History* (Bloomington: Indiana University Press, 2011).

Dontsov, Dmytro. 'Symon Petliura', *Literaturno Naukoyi Vistnyk* 7–8:5 (1926), 326–28.

Estraikh, Gennady. *In Harness: Yiddish Writers' Romance with Communism* (Syracuse: Syracuse University Press, 2005).

Estraikh, Gennady. *Soviet Yiddish: Language Planning and Linguistic Development* (Oxford: Clarendon Press, 1999).

Fishman, David E. *The Rise of Modern Yiddish Culture* (Pittsburgh: University of Pittsburgh Press, 2005).

Gilley, Christopher. 'Beyond Petliura: The Ukrainian National Movement and the 1919 Pogroms', *East European Jewish Affairs* 47:1 (2017), 45–61.

Gergel, Nokhem. 'The Pogroms in Ukraine in the Years 1918–1921' [English translation], *YIVO Annual of Jewish Social Science* 6 (1951), 237–52.

Gitelman, Zvi Y. *Jewish Nationality and Soviet Politics* (Princeton: Princeton University Press, 1972).

Gottesman, Itzik Nakhmen. *Defining the Yiddish Nation: the Jewish Folklorists of Poland* (Detroit: Wayne State University Press, 2003).

Greenbaum, Alfred Abraham. *Jewish Scholarship and Scholarly Institutions in Soviet Russia 1918–1953* (Jerusalem: The Hebrew University, 1978).

Gusev-Orenburgsky, Sergei. *Kniga o evreiskikh pogromakh na Ukraine v 1919 g.* [Book About Jewish Pogroms in Ukraine in 1919] (Petrograd: n.d.)

Hagen, William W. 'The Moral Economy of Ethnic Violence: The Pogrom in Lwow, November 1918', *Geschichte und Gesellschaft* 31:2 (2005), 203–26.

Taras Hunczak, 'A Reappraisal of Symon Petliura and Ukrainian-Jewish Relations, 1917–1921', *Jewish Social Studies* 31:3 (1969), 163–83.

Iekelchyk, Serhii. 'Trahichna storinka Ukrains'koi revoliutsii: Symon Petliura ta Ievreis'ki pogrom v Ukraini (1917–1920)', in Vasyl Mykhal'chuk (ed.), *Symon Petliura ta ukrains'ka natsional'na revoliutsiia* (Kyiv: Rada, 1995), pp. 165–217.

Jokusch, Laura. *Collect and Record: Jewish Holocaust Documentation in Early Postwar Europe* (Oxford: Oxford University Press, 2015).

Karlip, Joshua. *The Tragedy of a Generation: The Rise and Fall of Jewish Nationalism in Eastern Europe* (Cambridge, MA: Harvard University Press, 2013).

Kenez, Peter. 'Pogroms and White Ideology in the Russian Civil War', in John D. Klier and Shlomo Lambroza (eds.), *Pogroms: Anti-Jewish Violence in Modern Russian History* (Cambridge: Cambridge University, 1992), pp. 293–313.

Kenez, Peter. *Civil War in South Russia, 1919–1920* (Berkeley: University of California Press, 1977).

Kerler, Dov-Ber (ed.). *The Politics of Yiddish: Studies in Language, Literature, and Society* (Walnut Creek: Altamira, 1998).

Klier, John and Shlomo Lambroza. *Pogroms: Anti-Jewish Violence in Modern Russian History* (Cambridge: Cambridge University Press, 1992).

Krutikov, Mikhail. *From Kabbalah to Class Struggle: Expressionism, Marxism, and Yiddish Literature in the Life and Work of Meir Weiner* (Stanford: Stanford University Press, 2010).

Kuznitz, Cecile E. *YIVO and the Making of Modern Jewish Culture: Scholarship for the Yiddish Nation* (New York: Cambridge University Press, 2014).

Laqueur, Walter. *Black Hundred: The Rise of the Extreme Right in Russia* (New York: HarperCollins, 1993).

Magocsi, Paul Robert. *History of Ukraine: the Land and its Peoples* (Toronto: University of Toronto Press, 2010).

Miljakova, L. V. (ed.). *Kniga Pogromov: Pogromy na Ukraine, v Belorussii i Evropejskoi Chasti Rossii v Period Grazhdanskoi Voiny 1918–1922 gg.; Sbornik Dokumentov* (Moscow: ROSSPEN, 2007).

Motta, Giuseppe. *The Great War Against European Jewry 1914–1920* (Newcastle: Cambridge Scholars, 2017).

Peltz, Rakhmiel. 'The Undoing of Language Planning From the Vantage of Cultural History: Two Twentieth-Century Yiddish Examples', in Michael G. Clyne (ed.), *Undoing and Redoing Corpus Planning: Contributions to the Sociology of Language* (Berlin and New York: de Gruyter, 1997), pp. 327–56.

Polonsky, Antony. *The Jews in Poland and Russia, 1914–2008* (Oxford: The Littman Library of Jewish Civilization, 2010), III, pp. 32–43.

Schechtman, Joseph B. *Pogromy Dobrovolcheskoi Armii na Ukraine* [The Pogroms of the Volunteer Army in Ukraine] (Berlin: Ostjüdisches Historisches Archiv, 1932).

Shtif, Nokhem. *Di sotsyale diferentsyatsye in yidish: di hebreyishe elementn in der shprakh* [Social Differentiation in Yiddish: The Hebrew Elements of the Language], *Di yidishe shprakh* 17–18 (1929), 1–22.

Shtif, Nokhem. *Oytobiografye fun nokhem shtif* [The Autobiography of Nokhem Shtif] in *YIVO bleter* 5 (1933), 195–225.

Tcherikover, Elias [Tsherikover, Elye]. *Antisemitizm un pogromen in Ukrayne, 1917–1918* [Anti-Semitism and the Pogroms in Ukraine, 1917–1918] (Berlin: Yidisher literarisher ferlag, 1923).

Tcherikower, Elias. *Di Ukrainer pogromen in 1919* (New York: Yivo, 1965).

Trachtenberg, Barry. *The Revolutionary Roots of Modern Yiddish* (Syracuse: Syracuse University Press, 2008).

Weinreich, Max. 'Nokhem Shtif', *Di tsukunft* (New York) 38 (1933), 345–48.

Weinreich, Max. 'Vos volt yidish geven on hebreyish?' [What Would Yiddish Be Without Hebrew?], *Di tsukunft* (New York) 36 (1931), 194–205.

Weiser, Kalman. *Jewish People, Yiddish Nation: Noah Prylucki and the Folkists in Poland* (Toronto: University of Toronto Press, 2011).

נ. שטיף

פאגראמען
אין אוקראאינע

די צייט פון דער פרייוויליגער ארמיי

פארלאג "וואָסטאָק" בערלין C 2
An der Spandauer Brücke 2
1923

Frontispiece of the original Yiddish edition of Nokhem Shtif, *Pogromen in Ukrayne: di tsayt fun der frayviliger armey* (Berlin: Wostok, 1923)

The Pogroms in Ukraine:
The Period of the Volunteer Army[1]

Nokhem Shtif

Preface

I wrote this book in Kiev in March 1920, right after the Denikin atrocities that left a searing wound in our hearts and souls, even among those individuals and organizations who had been sympathetic to the Volunteer Army and who had hoped that it would be the "Angel of Deliverance" from Russia. They were all deceived, except for that small group of inveterate pessimists and those far-seeing activists who were struggling against that government. For the Jews of Ukraine it was a horrendous pogrom of murder and

---

1   The original Yiddish text, *Pogromen in Ukrayne: di tsayt fun der frayviliger armey* (Berlin: Wostok, 1923) has been digitized in the Steven Spielberg Digitized Yiddish Library on the website of the National Yiddish Book Center in Amherst, MA, which affirms: "National Yiddish Book Center respects the copyright and intellectual property rights in our books. To the best of our knowledge, this book is either in the public domain or it is an orphan work for which no copyright holder can be identified. If you hold an active copyright to this work — or if you know who does — please contact us by phone at 413–256–4900 x153, or by email at digitallibrary@bikher.org." The work is available online at https://s3.amazonaws.com/ingeveb/downloads/Shtif_Pogromen.pdf

Nota bene: Nokhem Shtif gives the dates of events using the Gregorian calendar adopted by the regime in 1918, sometimes followed by the Julian date.

All footnotes in this section are by the translator unless otherwise stated.

Translation © 2019 Maurice Wolfthal, CC BY 4.0   https://doi.org/10.11647/OBP.0176.03

devastation. The horrors of Ukraine in the year 1919 were unparalleled in the annals of pogroms. The bloody rampage has now subsided, and it is time to take stock.

At that time, my work had a specific purpose: to inform the world, and Jews in particular, of the destruction of the Jewish communities in Ukraine. As a member of the Editorial Board whose aim it was to collect and analyze documents concerning pogroms in Ukraine, I already had in my hands a quantity of materials on the pogroms committed by the Volunteer Army in 84 Jewish communities. My work rests on those documents. (I will discuss these materials more fully later. I am just summarizing here.) It soon becomes evident that the pogroms were indeed remarkably similar everywhere, when one considers how many took place in dozens of cities and towns. That is why I have avoided describing them individually: it would have meant endlessly repeating the same features. It seemed to me more useful, more informative, to outline the general characteristics of the main aspects, the typical pogrom activities of the Volunteer Army, and to discern a certain pattern from the details (the military character of the pogroms; the tortures; the mass rape of women; the total extermination of communities).

First I will describe the spectrum of pogroms, from the so-called "quiet pogroms" to the mass slaughters, and how they ebbed and flowed through the years. The pattern was so well established that when I returned to this subject in the Spring of this year with documentation on previously undocumented pogroms in 21 towns (and some more materials on pogroms already known), I did not have to change one thing, and I had nothing important to add. I simply had to enlarge the text under each rubric with additional details of the pogrom, and of course add the place where it occurred in the supplementary list at the end. This convinced me even more that I had correctly grasped the essence of the Denikin pogroms and that my method had been a good one, and my explanation became clearer and more concise. Enough said about the first, descriptive, part of the work.

The second part, "The Causes of the Pogroms," takes up two themes. First of all, it became necessary in the process of our effort, to explain exactly what had happened and the origins of those events. Second, we had to confirm such events if they were to be believed. Because it would be difficult for outsiders who had not experienced the horror themselves, and for those who were ignorant of the situation between Russia and Ukraine in general, to believe such atrocities if they were to read of the pogroms themselves, not linked to or entranced by the theory and practice of the Volunteer Army. Therefore we wanted to show that these pogroms were part of their military campaign, an integral part, tightly knitted — as bone to bone and flesh to flesh — to the whole military and political program of the Volunteer Army. Anyone who was familiar with its program would find it easy to believe the horrors of the pogroms, because these pogroms were not a secondary event. They were a link in a chain; that is what I have tried to demonstrate. The war aim of the Volunteer Army, of course, was to drive out the Bolshevik regime, and its social and political program aimed to restore every aspect of the old Russia before the days of the Revolution.

This was clearly evident in the way that the Denikin regime dealt with the three essential issues facing life in Russia: agriculture, labor, and the national question. These were their answers: The land must be returned to the aristocracy. The labor movement must be crushed. And complete Russification: we mock the national aspirations of the "alien tribes." In that program, Jews will continue to be second-class citizens, oppressed and subservient. This has been the logic of Reaction in every age and every land. Especially at those critical junctures when its power is in shaky and it is struggling to maintain its power, Reaction adds to this logic that Jews, all Jews without exception, are "enemies of the people" who must be dealt with harshly and severely with all possible means. And as soon as this is proclaimed, there begin, of course, attacks on the helpless, and "the wrath of the people" breaks out again. In Germany the German nationalists are screaming right now for what the Volunteer Army did three years ago in Ukraine.

For the reactionaries pogroms are a way to prevent Jews from obtaining equal rights, which the hated Revolution granted them. Pogroms are the first step towards reducing them to a state of slavery. That principle, which I propose in the second part of my book, is at the root of the pogroms. In the eyes of reactionaries Jews are creatures without rights. And as soon as anyone dares to give them their rights, they are outraged and they burn to "put the crown back on the head of perverted justice."

In the eyes of reactionaries, of course, Jews have no rights. They should not be politically active, and they must not have any Bolsheviks among them, so that no one might accuse them of any "outrages," because all the Jews are friends, and they are all responsible for each other. That has been the assumption of reactionaries for a long time. And that is the pogrom ideology of the Volunteer Army. It is an old story indeed. Nothing new or novel here, except for the Russian style and the Russian passion for finding things to bring back from the Dark Ages or from the atrocities of 1648 and 1760 in Ukraine.

The Volunteer Army contained elements of semi-civilized eastern peoples, Ossetians, Chechens, etc. and officers who were fortune-hunters. It had a poor war plan: a front with no objective and a demoralized rear. It had to be a marauding army that lived off plunder. Historical tradition pointed the pillagers against the Jews. The generals and politicians sat back and watched, and they were quietly pleased: it was all for the best that the Army obtain its own supplies, feed itself, and stock up on reserves. And they counted on this criminal mind-set to achieve another aim: to drive out the Bolsheviks and take Russia back. Those were the material conditions that gave rise to the pogroms. But the generals were wrong. The wave of pogroms in the end engulfed them, too, those who had quietly sat by and even encouraged them. The brutal massacres threw the Army into disarray and almost ruined it. The old historical rule came into play: Reaction is always blind and carries with it its own Angel of Death.

Of course, when I took up this work again, I was able to discuss these larger questions directly without getting mired in more voluminous detail. I believe that we did not need more. It seems to me that the reactionary character of the White Guard and its objectives are totally and completely clear to everyone who has watched the fate of Russia during the last four years. The shameful defeat of the Guard on every front demonstrates it one last time.

That part of my work, the most significant, was ready in the Spring of 1920. I am very grateful to no other than… V. V. Shulgin, the editor of *Kievlyanin*, the ideologist and defender of the Volunteer Army. He was extremely useful in helping me grasp the philosophy of the Volunteer Army, especially its program for the Jews and its zeal for pogroms. That outstanding publicist wrote so much on the subject in *Kievlyanin* that when you read Shulgin it is like reading the Army itself on the subject of the Jews, its theory and practice. Shulgin is certainly the greatest authority when it comes to anything relating to the Volunteer Army. He is its wise and trusted supporter. That was why I knew I could depend on his writings and rely on him, and on him alone. That was sufficient for my work.

This Spring I obtained a second reliable testimony. I am referring to K. N. Sokolov's unusual book, *The Regime of General Denikin* (Sofia, 1921).[2] K. N. Sokolov is a professor, an expert in government law, a minister in Denikin's regime, which is to say one who was politically active on behalf of the Volunteer Army and who remained true to the White dictatorship and its methods to the very end. Even after its ugly demise, he describes the dictatorship with an openness and a frankness (except on the agrarian debate over "commercial" topics) of which he can be proud. We have here, then, an authentic explanation, a piece of incontrovertible evidence concerning the program and the politics of Denikin's regime.

He did not add much to what we can learn from reading Shulgin. But for my work it was important that an authentic participant like K. N. Sokolov confirmed almost everything that I had said earlier about the essential nature of the Volunteer Army, its political theory and practice, and also about the roots and growth of its pogrom activities. I have taken some passages from Sokolov's book on the principles and practice of the Volunteer Army on the most important issues in Russian life, and some that confirm Shulgin's writings and my hypotheses. I was pleased that my earlier writing was thus corroborated. I considered V. V. Shulgin and K. N. Sokolov to be such iron-clad witnesses on the fundamental political aims of the Volunteer Army and on the Jewish question, that I did not require any more evidence to bring this work to completion. But in its present form, having analyzed the whole Volunteer system, I have gone beyond my original intention, and I believe it is ready to be presented to a broader audience of readers.

Here are just a few words on the nature of the documentation that I have used in the first, descriptive, part. It is original material, both because it has never been published before, and because it was collected for a specific purpose according to a certain format. The aim was historical, not political. The Editorial Board mentioned above was not aimed at the short term, but at the perspective of history. Its mission

---

2   K. N. Sokolov, *Pravlenie generala Denikina: iz vospominanij* (Sofia: Rossijsko-Bolgarskoe Knigoizdat, 1921).

was to collect everything in connection with the pogroms in Ukraine starting in 1917: everything that victims, witnesses, and researchers saw or heard, reported as accurately as possible, official documents of government, institutions, organizations, etc. — all material for a large historical work. The greatest merit of this documentation is that it has absolutely nothing to do with newspaper sensationalism or party politics.

The material is varied both as to the questions asked and as to its source. On the subject of a pogrom (or more accurately, pogroms) that occurred in the same place, there are often parallel documents assembled by different organizations, along different themes and using different methods. That in itself constitutes a verification of the facts under discussion. Furthermore there was verification within the Editorial Board itself, whose members would often meet with victims and with witnesses who had been compelled to flee in such large numbers to Kiev from many devastated towns, as well as with the correspondents and researchers for the editors. In addition, over the course of working for two years in Ukraine, the Board had accrued enough experience to have developed a feel for the accounts of the witnesses and informants.

But it must be said that with respect to materials specifically in connection with the Volunteer Army, something stands out that makes them credible even if there were no strict verification: the very fact that huge numbers of reports are extremely similar. When hundreds of people from different places describe the pogroms in almost the exact same way, using the same words (and this cannot be said of accounts of pogroms by Petliura's men or by bandits), that means that they are to be essentially believed. Either that or this is a case of mass hysteria, or they have all been prompted.

There is, finally, a quantity of documents: orders, announcements, decrees, etc., from local and central authorities; protocols; reports and memoranda of various organizations that were sympathetic to the Volunteer Army; lists of those who were murdered; reports from doctors who treated the wounded, etc. We thus have accumulated a unique collection of materials that will meet the strictest scholarly standards. If all this documentation were to be published, the world would be shocked. But I think that the little bit of material that I present here in a compressed summary, will be sufficiently convincing.

There is one great formal drawback to this material: we have only one side. We have heard and seen the oppressed but not the oppressors. That a Jewish commission would seek out the views of the oppressors on their thoughts and actions is almost unimaginable. But I am sure that even if that were possible, we would obtain more that was noteworthy from the psychological point of view, not the historical. The oppressed have reported enough on the events that is historical, objective, and credible.

We have such rare testimony from V. V. Shulgin and K. N. Sokolov — spokesmen and leaders of the oppressors — on the meaning and purpose of the pogroms, and on the link between those events and the essence and philosophy of the Volunteer Army, that we need look no further.

Berlin. July 17, 1922

I. The Situation of the Jews in Ukraine Before the Arrival of Denikin's Volunteer Army

Anarchy and Pogroms

Since the Ukrainian nationalist movement began to campaign openly for an independent state (*samostinost*) at the end of 1917, but mainly since December 1918, when the Directorate[3] — Vynnychenko,[4] Petliura,[5] Shvets,[6] Andriievskyi,[7] and Makarenko[8] — organized the revolt against Hetman Skoropadskyi,[9] the land has not ceased to be a field for military operations. The bloody battle for power has not abated. The land seethes and sinks into anarchy and decay. Before that time, before the Denikin era, the land had gone through three regimes: the independent Ukrainian People's Republic with the Central Rada and with the General-Secretariat, at the end of 1917; the brief Bolshevik regime, Pyatakov's government,[10] January–February 1918; fictional independence with the restored Central Rada, actually under German occupation, March–April 1918; the Hetmanate, a similar fiction under German rule, May–December 1918; the Ukrainian Directorate, end

---

3   Provisional committee organized by the Ukrainian National Union to overthrow Pavlo Skoropadskyi's Hetmanate.

4   Volodymyr Vynnychenko: member of the Ukrainian Revolutionary Party and first Prime Minister under the General Secretariat, then member of the Directorate.

5   Symon Petliura: Supreme Commander of the army of the Ukrainian National Republic that was established in 1917 and chairman of the Directorate formed in 1918.

6   Fedir Shvets: Geology professor, elected to the Central Committee of the Peasants' Union and the Socialist Revolutionary Party, then the Directorate.

7   Opanas Andriievskyi: representative of the militaristic Ukrainian Party of Socialist-Independentists in the Directorate.

8   Andrii Makarenko: representative of the Railway Workers' Union in the Directorate.

9   Pavlo Skoropadskyi: General in the Russian Army, then the Ukrainian National Army, who in 1918 overthrew the provisional government and declared himself hetman. Was himself overthrown by the Directorate under Petliura.

10   Yuriy Pyatakov: a founder and leader of the Ukrainian Communist (Bolshevik) Party.

of December 1918–February 1919; the Ukrainian Soviet Republic, the Bolsheviks in power, February–August 1919.

General Denikin and staff (1916). Photographer unknown. Library of Congress, digital ID ggbain.29429. Wikimedia, https://commons.wikimedia.org/wiki/File: Gen._Denikin_%26_staff_LCCN2014709587.tif

But as different as these regimes were, they still shared some characteristics: 1) The land was fragmented under all the regimes, like a political chessboard of various powers. 2) The regimes were military, under constant mobilization. 3) The regimes were very weak.[11]

None of the regimes that considered themselves central or national ever actually controlled all of Ukraine. In various border areas, and even in the middle of the territory of a regime, that regime often competed with other "authorities" that "captured" and controlled their own provinces, districts, and counties, and considered themselves a government. This situation was especially notable before the second Soviet regime (February–August 1919). Parallel to the Ukrainian Soviet Republic (the Kiev regime) there existed at various times and in various combinations, Petliura's Republic in parts of the provinces Volhynia and Podolia, Makhno's and Grigoriev's governments; not to mention territories that smaller partisan military units and criminal gangs had seized, led by the Atamans Zelenyi,[12] Sokolovsky, Angel,[13] Tiutiunik,[14]

---

11 There was one exception. In this aspect the German occupation was stronger and better organized, but not totally [note by the author].
12 Danylo Terpilo.
13 Yevgeni Petrovych.
14 Yurii Tiutiunik.

Struk,[15] and others, who waged war under various flags or under no flag at all, primarily to plunder and "go wild" without interference.

This political chessboard of an assortment of "authorities" battling for control over territory meant that each regime had to be above all a military organization capable of attracting Ukrainians and to maintain its power by waging war against its enemies on all fronts. Under such conditions it was impossible for a central government to really practice statecraft, to organize the economy and civil life. And the longer these military operations continued, the worse was the devastation of the land, exponentially.

Add to this situation the real weakness of the regimes. Not one of them, because of their short duration and other organic reasons, managed to take root and dominate the land. Not one managed to accomplish anything substantial for the people, while at the same time they demanded their manpower and their last bit of money. Not one of them was rooted in the way of life and political traditions of the population. That was why they all had to rely almost purely on military power and punitive expeditions. That was why each regime did not really govern except in the larger centers where it had its military power and garrisons, and only when that military was not in retreat. This was true even within its own territory, or better said, on territory that no other authority was claiming for itself.

Smaller towns and villages were left vulnerable. Every village that had been armed from head to toe in the World War was on a war-footing against every authority, resisted every government discipline, and readily helped every new power overthrow the last. The same villages provided the Directorate with an army to overthrow the Hetman and the Germans; helped the Bolsheviks against the Directorate; supplied Petliura with units and partisans against the Soviet authorities; and were a constant source of adventurists and criminal gangs. Through all these regimes, Ukraine gave the impression of a patchwork of republics and dictatorships, or better said, of innumerable military fronts. Three main movements were involved on these fronts in various entanglements: Ukrainian nationalism (*samostiniks*), Soviet Communism, and Anarchist banditry. Across the length and breadth of the whole country, from north to south, from west to east and back, regular military troops

---

15   Ilya Timofeyevich Struk [note by the author].

were constantly on the march and armed gangs were on the move, overrunning helpless towns and villages like a torrential flood with artillery fire and the most savage atrocities, shredding the last vestiges of a peaceable culture and a normal way of life.

It was a landscape of decay and ruination, with depressed and hungry towns that flocked like sheep to any pastor with a gun and lawless villages that no regime could subdue. It was not difficult to foresee that under such bloody circumstances, the Jews, unarmed observers standing by, would be passive victims, in particular within the Ukrainian tradition of pogroms. But the events that took place were far worse than anything that had been imagined. The war of the Directorate against the Hetmanate, and then against the Bolsheviks, which followed soon after, brought with it military pogroms in Ovruch, Korosten, Zhitomir, Proskurov, and Felshtin that made the pogroms in Ukraine of the previous fifty years pale by comparison, judging by the number of people murdered, and by their cruelty and savagery.

Ovruch Pogrom (February 1919). Photographer unkonown. Wikimedia, https://commons. wikimedia.org/wiki/File:OvruchPogrom.png

The situation grew even worse during the period of the Soviet regime. Petliura's military campaign, and in addition the brutal guerilla war waged against the Soviets by various gangs, plus the involvement of local hooligans and bandits — all contributed to a state of permanent pogrom in Ukraine.

Petliura's detachments, Makhno's, Grigoriev's, and other units exterminated hundreds of Jewish communities and settlements. Many little towns were completely wiped out, or the few remaining Jewish survivors fled. Tens of thousands of Jews were murdered in the most barbaric way. Even more were wounded, and many were permanently crippled. A large proportion of Jews in Ukraine have been reduced to begging, depending on the help of the Committee.[16] Even worse than the economic ruin was the feeling of bleak despair. Helpless communities, like peaceful islands amid a sea of armed military people, lived in constant fear of death or losing their last few possessions. A little Jewish town that had been plundered and battered ten times was constantly aware that the murderer's axe might strike any day, any time.

The Economic Pogrom

The pogroms, of course, destroyed the economic well-being of many Jews in Ukraine, but there were other factors, too, that had undermined it. Industry came to an end during this civil war, following four years of World War. The country went from well-developed commerce to a primitive economy, bartering a shirt for forty pounds of potatoes, and business turned into speculation. Some became rich at the expense of hundreds of thousands of ruined people. The country, which had been closely connected commercially to Russia and to the world, suddenly became isolated. It broke down into fragmented, parceled, territories all at war with each other. And they all degenerated side by side, with no trains, no industry, no commerce. On the roads Jews were again vulnerable to the mortal dangers of medieval highways. The towns became parasites. They lost their economic function, and the villages settled scores with the cities. Such conditions were disastrous for Jews, many of whom were businessmen, tradesmen, craftsmen, and managers, who needed a developed system of trade as much as air to breathe; a vibrant exchange with distant markets; flexible credit; etc. — the whole mechanism of a free and undisturbed capitalist system.

In addition, the Soviet agenda — the prohibition of commerce, the nationalization of the vast majority of industrial enterprises, the requisitions, the taxes — the whole economic war against the bourgeoisie, also helped ruin Jewish residents who lived mostly from trade and industry. In a little Jewish town the "bourgeois" was the owner of a little seltzer-water factory who owned his own little house, or the little shopkeeper, etc. The huge masses of Jews who lost their

---

16   The All-Ukrainian Relief Committee for the Victims of Pogroms.

regular jobs and could not manage to adapt to Soviet rule had to live off the wind, resorting to smalltime speculation that was very dangerous, or to selling off their household goods, or to living off the kindness of their children who could find jobs under the Soviets.

Hopes for the Volunteer Army

It was therefore inevitable that when the Volunteer Army took over Ukraine in August 1919, the vast majority of Jews, more than other segments of the population, would welcome with joy and devotion any new regime that might restore safety and a peaceful existence. Who else had felt so deceived by all the previous regimes? Who else had suffered so many murders, massacres, and mortal fear? Who else was as much economically and emotionally depressed? And who else had longed, as much as the vast majority of Jews, for "law and order?" In retrospect it is difficult now to grasp, but in fact at the time when the Volunteer Army was starting to take over Ukraine, a large number of Jews looked upon it as though it were the Angel of Deliverance. And it is certainly true that among the Jewish delegations that went to receive the Army with bread and salt, this was not hypocrisy or just a despondent people asking meekly for mercy from the new authorities, but also a sincere enthusiasm for an authority that would bring "law and order." They believed and they hoped, and they were ready to help and serve the Volunteer Army as best they could.

The political friends of the Volunteer Army among the bourgeoisie at home and abroad ceaselessly proclaimed that it would be a regime that established "law and order," and that it would support a Constituent Assembly, a democracy, proper and rightful, with the working class and with Jews. At a time when cities and towns in Ukraine were isolated and disconnected from each other, and each Jewish community was practically a government unto itself, and there was very little news was available, and nothing from the other side of the front, under such circumstances the Jews had almost no information about the "excesses" and massacres that the Volunteer Army had already committed in June and July of 1919.

Even the Bolshevik press, which warned that this would be a Monarchist — Black Hundreds regime, made no special mention of pogroms committed against Jews. Almost every city and every town had to learn the bitter truth only by living through it. They learned it too late, but until then a large proportion of Jews had hoped and wished that an army that could "liberate Russia," and that stood for a united nation and a Constituent Assembly — according to Admiral Kolchak's declaration — and that had shown such energy during the war — such an army would be strong enough to establish a government and put an end to civil war, and was possessed of enough statecraft to protect the peaceful communities, or at the least, not perpetrate pogroms itself.

What else could a community like Bohuslav (Kiev province), have expected, where the pogrom went as follows: "On April 4, 1919, the partisans drove out the Bolsheviks and came into town. They pillaged and robbed all the Jews. They murdered twenty and wounded about fifty. Then our town became an encampment and suffered heavy artillery almost every day. On May 12 the Bolsheviks retreated. The partisans attacked again and murdered several more Jews, again robbed everyone, pillaging clothes and housewares. Finally on May 13 they set fire to Jewish houses and shops. They burned down fifty homes, 100 shops and stores, and seven houses of worship." The very same account could have been reported by dozens and dozens of Jewish communities. Just change the name of the perpetrators to: Petliura's Cossacks,[17] Grigoriev's army, Struk's bandits, etc. The Jews soon realized that black days were facing them, and that the hoped-for Volunteer Army was surpassing the worst pogroms in the history of Ukraine.

---

17   Don Cossacks and Kuban Cossacks.

II. Before the Pogroms and During the Pogroms

The Pogrom Road

We can now say with certainty that the strategic path of the Volunteer Army was the pogrom road, from its victory march of June–October 1919 to the terrified retreat before the Bolsheviks in November 1919–January/ February 1920. "Such-and-such unit of the Volunteer Army arrived and committed a pogrom and left with a pogrom," is the same formula that summarizes the reports of news from the vast majority of communities: Bobrovytsia (Chernihiv province); Bohuslav, Horodyshche, Korsun, Cherkasy, Smila (Kiev province); Tomashpil (Podolia province), etc. Wherever the Volunteer Army set foot, the Jewish communities suffered savage murders, massacres, and rapes. The Volunteer road mainly followed the train lines, its general strategy being to continue the civil war, with no specific frontline, but rather along the railroads and waterways.

So as soon as the Volunteer Army took a train station, especially a junction, it meant that the other side — the Bolsheviks or Petliura's army — immediately ceded an area to the east or to the north, which was taken without a battle. In this way large parcels of territory were conquered automatically merely by taking particular train junctions. Huge tracts of land, therefore, were won without the use of weapons. That territory was conquered quietly, without battle, by the police and the militias. Because of that, and because the commanders of the Volunteer Army were very impatient to use all their strength to seize the center, Moscow, as soon as possible, they left the rear of the army unprotected. As a result not every Jewish community in Ukraine suffered Denikin's pogroms. There simply were no Volunteer Army units there, no pogromists.

The Volunteer Army crisscrossed through Ukraine on the railroad lines running from east to west: down the middle from Rostov to Kiev, through Kharkiv, Poltava, Ramodan; along the north through

Sumy, Konotop, and Niezhyn (Chernihiv province); along the south through Znamenka and Fastiv. And on the side lines that connect the administrative centers (especially the line between Bakhmach and Cherkasy), on the line running north from Kiev to the Chernihiv district, on the line running south to the Kiev-Volyn area, where they forced Petliura's army to the Kiev-Kozyatyn line. A glance at these routes gives us a picture of the geography of the pogroms.

The worst devastation occurred precisely at these rail centers: Konotop, Niezhyn, Bobrovytsia, Kremenchug, Cherkasy, Khorol, Pryluk, Bila-Tserkava, Fastiv, etc. or very near these train stations: Kaniv, Stepanets, Bohuslav, Mezhyrich, Rossovo, Tagancha, Hostomel, Makarov (Kiev province); Borzna, Novy-Malyn, Ostior (Chernihiv province). The converse is also true: historians of Denikin's expedition will be able to easily trace the Volunteer Army's movements, victories, and defeats by following the bloody tracks of its pogroms.

The Ebb and Flow of the Wave of Pogroms

Types of Pogroms

The wave of pogroms increased as the Volunteer Army advanced deeper into Jewish territory, those areas where the Jewish population was in the majority in the cities and towns, especially in Kiev province. The Army felt the need to celebrate victories, to confirm their hope and certainty of winning the war. They were constantly being incited into a savage hatred of the Jews. The attitude towards pogroms was very clear that Jews were worthless, and there was no need to fear punishment. Under such circumstances, pogroms increased, and took on new targets and new tactics. Three stages can be discerned:

1. The period of "quiet pogroms," as we might call them, mostly in Kharkiv, Poltava, and Yekaterinoslav provinces. It meant assaults against individual people. Every day people were attacked and beaten, and a few Jewish homes were plundered. But since it dragged on for months (for example in Kharkiv, Yekaterinoslav, Kiev), it victimized the whole Jewish community. The main purpose was quick robbery, especially

of money, jewelry, valuables. Murders were few, and they tried to excuse those by claiming that only Communists were being targeted or their sympathizers. The worst part of these "quiet pogroms" was the rape of Jewish women. The longer the pogrom lasted, the more women were raped. This was notably true in Yekaterinoslav.

2. The period of mass pogroms, in the eastern part of Poltava province, in the southern part of Chernihiv province, and the eastern part of Kiev province. During two or three days the entire Jewish population was systematically attacked and plundered. They went from house to house, pillaging everything, taking shirts right off people and their last shoes. They plundered the houses completely, from pianos to kitchen utensils, as well as the stores. They loaded everything onto wagons and took it all home to their lodgings on "the quiet Don." They would hold an auction for some of the things, and sold them for change to Christians from town or from nearby. In addition, they would destroy any Jewish possessions that they could not steal or sell. They would burn some of their houses and shops, and murder them a few at a time. Sometimes they would extort huge bribes to let them live, especially with "Nikolayev" money. They raped Jewish women en masse.

3. The period of bloody pogroms, or slaughters in Kiev and Chernihiv provinces at the end of August and September 1919, and in Podolia province while retreating until February 1920. Such pogroms were perpetrated first in locales that changed hands many times in succession, like Borzna which changed hands five times. They were taking revenge for recent defeats, and the fabricated excuse was that Jews had shot at the Volunteer Army from their homes and hidden places. This occurred in Niezhyn, Borzna, Konotop, and Novy-Malyn (Chernihiv province) and Fastiv (Kiev province). It occurred mainly on their retreat in Krivoye-Ozero, Tomashpil (Podolia province), and some places in Kiev province. These were mass murders of the Jewish residents who could not hide or escape, in the most barbaric ways: 600 souls in Fastiv, and about the

same number in Krivoye-Ozero.[18] They could not ransom their lives. Complete devastation, arson, and rape were the rule.

There was a little variation in the course of the pogroms, both as to their duration and as to the excuses that were fabricated. For example, no excuse was made for the slaughter in Rossovo (Kiev province), on August 28, 1919, as soon as the Volunteer Army took the town. But as a rule the pogroms of the Volunteer Army followed the same pattern.

There were some changes after the mass murders of September 1919, probably due to new situations on the frontlines. The murderous energy of the Volunteer Army faltered as the Bolsheviks strengthened their position in the western part of Kiev province along the Irpen River to Berdychiv and further, and in the northern part of Chernihiv province. They began to drive out the Volunteer Army. The Poles controlled the western part of Volyn and Podolia provinces, part of Galicia (the Vinnytsia district). The south, in Kherson province and part of Podolia, where Baron Schilling's army was operating, was disconnected from north Ukraine, because in the middle — in Yekaterinoslav province and also in Tovarish — Ataman Makhno was attacking. The powers that had ruled Ukraine were now being expelled to the north and the east. Most of the fighting was taking place in the Russian provinces, where there were small Jewish agricultural settlements on the roads to Moscow,[19] with attacks by Mamontov[20] and Shkuro.[21] When they were finished with the more recent communities, they turned on the long-established ones that had already suffered pogroms. The wave of massacres ebbed into "quiet pogroms."

A new wave erupted with the shattering of the Volunteer Army in a terrified rout before the Red Army. They committed pogroms a second time, a third, a fourth, in parts of Kiev province: December 1919: Horodyshche, Cherkasy, Smila, Stavyshche, Monastyryshche, Tetiiv, and others. Part of Bredov's[22] army tried to break through to Rumania,

---

18   Elias Heifetz, in his *The Slaughter of the Jews in Ukraine* (New York: Thomas Seltzer, 1921), p. 111, puts the number murdered in Fastiv at 1,500–1,800.

19   These settlements were not ignored, and there were slaughters in Balashov on 14 July, in Kozlov and Yelets, 31 August/7 September, in Oriol and others [note by the author].

20   Konstantin Mamontov.

21   Andrei Grigorevich Shkuro.

22   Nikolai Bredov: lieutenant-general in the Russian army and a commander of the Volunteer Army.

but they were stopped, so they turned back and perpetrated pogroms in Podolia Province. January–February 1920: Tomashpil, Yampol, Miaskova, Dzhurin, Yaruga, Verbka, and others. And at the end of April 1920, when Petliura launched a new attack in Ukraine with the Poles, we find the old pogromists, the few remnants of Denikin's Don Cossacks and Kuban Cossacks[23] again slaughtering in Kalyus (Podolia province), this time in the service of Petliura or the Poles!

Hostages

Before going into a description of the pogrom activities of the Volunteer Army, and its disastrous effects on Jewish life, one aspect of the Army's treatment of the Jews is worth noting because it is characteristic of its whole campaign of pogroms. I am referring to the seizing of Jewish hostages. They resurrected this tactic, which the old Tsarist regime had tried and abandoned during the World War. Its purpose, like that of other outrages, had been to demonstrate that "the Jews are the enemies of Russia," and they must be reduced to their old status of servility and submission.

On June 18 and 19, they seized eleven people as hostages in Valk (Kharkiv province): Shlessberg, a watchmaker; Glikin a tailor; Katz, a student; Brandes, a woman; a doctor, and others. The fabricated pretext was that when the Bolsheviks had retreated from various locales, they had taken hostages from the upper class, although without regard to nationality, Jews and Christians alike. Five of the Jewish hostages worked alongside their Russian co-workers in gardens that members of the Kharkiv Vegetarian Society had planted. A spokesman for that group, Grigory Khvostaty, stood up for those hostages, and was told: "We have nothing against your gardeners, only against a certain nationality." The second in command added: "All kikes are Bolsheviks. You can slash them and murder them." They shot one of the hostages, Glikin, on June 20. Shlessberg went insane. The rest were let go on July 1. The Volunteer Army was then starting to launch its military operations. Everywhere they were proclaiming that it was democratic and would

---

23   Historically, numerous Cossacks from the Don and Kuban region fought in cavalry regiments in the Russian army under the Tsar, as well as in the 'White' armies during the Civil War against the Bolsheviks.

treat all the nationalities of Russia equally, and the commanders realized that hostage-taking wasn't appropriate. But the simple Cossack and officer, who took no interest in politics, found a better way to keep "the enemies" terrorized: a pogrom.

The Welcome

It has already been noted that after the rule of the Bolsheviks, some Jews of the business and industrial class were ready to welcome the Volunteer Army as "their own" regime, which would restore a climate of private ownership and commerce. But even the majority of Jews, going against their economic interests and political sympathies, were terrified and depressed by unending pogroms, and naively hoped that the Volunteer Army would be a pillar of "law and order" and would certainly establish a "strong hand" to save the Jews from pogroms. That is why it was common that the Volunteer Army was welcomed warmly, and delegations were sent to greet them with bread and salt. They offered them food and raised sums of money were for the Army.

But even then, right at the start, their disappointment was bitter. We will mention just a few examples among many. On August 25, 1919, in Boryspil (Poltava province) a Jewish delegation came out three times to welcome their honored guests. They asked to meet with the commander, but received this reply: "Bread and salt will not help you, Jewish murderers!" On September 13, a reconnaissance unit approached Bobrovytsia. Jews and Christians went to meet them, and the Jews were thankful that the threat of a pogrom no longer hung over them from one of Romashko's gangs who were active in the area. But now they heard, "What are the kikes so happy about? Our men are coming, and we'll butcher them all." And, as elsewhere, they were prepared to fulfill their promise. They began to plunder and rape and murder Jews. Nor was money of any use when the military attacked a Jewish home at dinner time on October 17 in Pavoloch (Kiev province). And it didn't help any that they generously fed the Cossacks in Fastiv.

The Jewish delegation in Korsun met a harrowing end. The Bolsheviks had fled on August 24. The town learned that a unit of the Terek Plastun Brigade was 8 or 10 versts away at Razodovka village. A delegation of four Christians and three Jews went to meet them and to welcome them to their town. On August 25 a small group of Cossacks arrived. Christians and Jews led by the rabbi greeted them. A meeting was held. Speeches were made, and assurances were given that the peaceful residents had nothing to fear; there would be no massacres; the inhabitants should remain calm and friendly, etc. The next day, on August 26, local Bolsheviks retook the town for a few hours. Two of the Jewish delegation (Scheinblum and Slavutsky) were murdered, because they had been sympathetic to the Volunteer Army. The third man went into hiding.

Later that day a unit of the Plastun Brigade arrived and drove out the Bolsheviks, and they immediately began a slaughter. The rabbi, who had welcomed the Volunteer Army just the day before, was murdered in the most savage way. He was literally ripped apart. In general the pogroms started with the delegation. On August 29th, in Kaharlik (Kiev province) they greeted the Jewish delegation graciously. But the officer had barely turned away when his men attacked them and robbed them of everything. In the little town of Kobyzhcha (Chernihiv province) they attacked the Jewish delegation, which had come to the train station, and stole everything from them, stripped them naked from head to toe, and beat them. The town of Makarov, which had 4,000 Jewish souls, had already suffered through a series of pogroms from June to the end of August at the hands of local gangs. Most of the Jews had fled, leaving about 200 old men and women. They sent a delegation of 17 white-haired elderly people. Not one of them returned. They had been hacked to pieces.

Pogroms

As has been noted, in many cases they began with the delegations, as a signal to start. A military unit comes to town, usually Cossacks, and they spread out in groups of 5, 6, or 10 men, often with officers. They rob and beat Jews who happen to be on the street, they strip them naked, shoot them and slash them with swords, and force the unfortunates to show them where there are richer Jews, and Jews in general. In many cases local hooligans join in, they lead the way and are thrown a bone from the bloody meal. They demand money from the Jews in their homes, especially "Nikolayev," and jewelry, gold, and silver. Terrified Jews, who have already suffered through earlier pogroms, waste no time in spreading out on the table everything that is in their pockets and chest of drawers.

And the Cossacks immediately pack everything into their bags and sacks. They take everything down to the last shirt. But they're not satisfied with that, and demand what has been hidden away. They terrorize them into revealing what is hidden and where, by inflicting the most cruel savagery, like lynchings. But they won't believe them, and rip apart ovens, walls, floors, and bedspreads. They destroy attics and cellars and dig up yards. If they're still not satisfied with their plunder, or if they find something hidden, they torture them and threaten them with death and pretend to shoot them, and then extort huge sums to let them live. And they tell them to borrow the money from their Christian neighbors.

In the midst of all this horror — as women and children are wailing and weeping, as the wounded are moaning, as windows are being smashed, furniture is ripped apart, ovens are being trashed, and walls are torn down — they start raping the women right in front of their parents, husbands, and children, and then leave the area. They pay no mind to the parents. Pleading and crying are of no use. Every attempt at resistance by the woman or the others ends with murder. Often they drag the women away with them. When they're finished, they take all the Jewish possessions and pack them onto wagons, their own or those of farmers, or in trucks, take them to the station and load up the train cars. Sometimes, as in Bila-Tserkava, they turn the plunder over to their women who have come with them from the Don and the Kuban to watch. They smash whatever they do not want or cannot take with them, like furniture, or give it to local hooligans and farmers who have come prepared with wagons and sacks. And again they attack the homes, breaking down doors, windows, ovens. They turn the houses into ruins, when they don't just burn them down.

One group leaves and another comes, then a third, etc., each one taking what has been left behind. Each time they again demand money, jewelry, etc. They rage like wild beasts, beating and torturing, stabbing and shooting at those who have not managed to escape and hide the first time around. They hunt down the Jews, who run through the streets from house to house, almost naked and barefoot, half-crazed, desperately looking for a place to hide, a hole, a field, a woods. The best they hope for is to hide with a Christian neighbor. But not for long, because the rumor spreads that Christians may not hide Jews, and even a good Christian pleads with the Jew to leave, or just throws him out. This "wildness" can last "legally" for three days, the Cossacks report, but sometimes goes longer, sometimes shorter, depending on how long it takes to finish the job.

During all this there are some desperate and daring Jews who struggle to find their way to "the authorities" to make their accusations. First they get a lecture: "Kikes are commissars"... all Jews are Bolsheviks... Jews have ruined Russia... Jews are the enemies of the Volunteer Army. Then they are insulted and thrown out, depending on the personal whim of the local commander, the garrison chief, etc. They are advised to offer a generous bribe to the Cossacks, and nothing more will happen, because "Measures have already been taken." But it is obvious from the words of "the authorities," and it is made abundantly clear, that nothing can be done because the Cossacks are "extremely angry" with Jewish Bolsheviks, and "they are right." Sometimes the order is given that "violent acts" against peaceful residents must stop. But these "measures" and "orders" have this in common: no one pays attention to them. The pogrom criminals know "the authorities" well, and they laugh at their paper displeasure and their paper threats. The pogroms run their course until their natural end: when there is nothing more to pillage, nothing left to destroy. Usually the order to stop comes after it is all done. There was a case in Bila-Tserkava, where Colonel Sakharov proclaimed an order banning pogroms on September 1, 1919, two weeks after the pogrom had begun.

After a few days, the remaining survivors crawl out of their hideouts and start collecting the corpses of the murdered in the houses, the attics, and the cellars, and on the streets where the dogs and pigs have ripped them apart. They bury them in mass graves and pay their last respects. Sometimes when Jews gather for this tragic ceremony, it becomes another opportunity to take revenge on "the Bolsheviks," to steal their last pair of boots, to rape the women, etc. At such a funeral in Bobrovytsia they raped the 15-year-old daughter of the caretaker at the cemetery. Finally "things quiet down," as the commanders write in their reports.

The "quiet pogrom" now replaces the mass pillage and murders. Jews are robbed on the street and in their homes. As soon as the sun sets, the town becomes deathly quiet. There are no Jews on the street. Dozens of families gather in the few houses that are still intact, so as to get through the terror together, through the awful nights. They lock themselves in, they bolt the doors and gates and listen for every sound. In this deadly silence they can hear rifle shots here and there, followed by terrible screams. They come from a house that has been attacked and from the neighbors: banging, drumming, whistling — a primitive way to let "the authorities" know and to scare away the murderers.

We have an account of that terror and those harrowing screams in the black of night, related with the highest level of credibility.[24] It was described by none other than V. V. Shulgin, editor of *Kievlyanin*, a highly-placed source, the true ideologue of the pogrom campaign. He certainly has no interest in exaggerating the massacres by his Volunteer Army. He writes: "At night a medieval terror reigns in the streets of Kiev. In the empty streets and the deathly quiet heart-rending screams can be heard. It is the "kikes" who are screaming. They are screaming in terror. On a dark street somewhere a mob of people with knives rushes through apartment buildings from top to bottom. Whole streets, overcome with terror, are screaming with horrendous voices fearing for their lives. It is terrifying to hear these voices… harrowing, a veritable Inquisition that the whole Jewish community is experiencing."[25] At that time V. V. Shulgin was living in a Jewish neighborhood in Kiev, incidentally not far from the commander-in-chief of the Kiev district, General [Vladimir Mikhailovich] Dragomirov. He certainly heard plenty of "those harrowing screams," especially on the nights of October 17–22, 1919, and we can trust him. He modestly veils the atrocities of those "people with knives," and, incidentally, he draws a moral lesson from this horrendous tragedy, both for him and for the Jews. We will discuss this more later.

So it grows "quiet" until the next occasion. For example, a military unit leaves and another comes in its stead; or there's a defeat on the front; or the Bolsheviks take a town for a while and then they are

---

24 Richard Pipes estimates that 300 Jews were murdered in this "quiet pogrom." See *Russia Under the Bolshevik Regime* (New York: Knopf, 1993), p. 108.

25 'The Terror Inquisition,' *Kievlyanin*, No. 37, dated 8/21 October 1919 [note by the author].

driven out, and are forced to retreat. Pogroms erupt each time with increasing ferocity. These repeat pogroms are often the bloodiest, the most horrendous.

In such cases it develops in a state of permanent pogrom that can last for weeks or months as in Bobrovytsia, Borzna, Niezhyn (Chernihiv province); Bohuslav, Bila-Tserkava, Fastiv, Cherkasy (Kiev province); and others. It was most savage when they took over a town and when they left it, and in between there was a "quiet pogrom." In the larger cities, like Kharkiv, Yekaterinoslav, and Kiev, it was mostly a "quiet pogrom" with mass slaughter only on occasion. Kiev suffered such mass pogroms on October 17–22, when the Volunteer Army was beaten by the Reds and then took back the city, under the eyes of General Dragomirov, their supreme commander, General Bredov, the military leader, and other "authorities."

The permanent pogrom ebbs or stops for a while only in two situations: either when the Cossacks leave, or when the last remaining Jews escape. Whole Jewish communities that could no longer bear the Inquisition and living in mortal fear, and had nothing more to lose, took the elderly and the children and the sick and set out on foot wherever the dangerous road would take them, usually to the nearest Jewish community, which had been devastated and turned to ruins, just like their own.

III. The Volunteer Army's Own Style of Pogrom

Before the period of the Volunteer Army, Ukraine had already experienced many pogroms of various types, by Petliura's military units, Atamans, and ordinary bandits. Nevertheless the Volunteer Army managed to be innovative, adding something new of its own that made it stand out from the earlier pogroms. The most prominent features of its style were: 1) its military character 2) the mass rape of women 3) special humiliations and tortures 4) the extermination of entire Jewish communities. In that aspect its only rivals were the slaughters by the Cossacks in the 17th and 18th centuries during the eras of Khmelnytsky (1648) and Gonta (1768).

The Military Character of the Pogroms. Relations with the Local Population

Local Christians had taken part in the earlier pogroms of 1919, mostly the ignorant peasants and the reactionary wing of the intelligentsia, particularly those who felt they had been harmed by the Revolution; former officials from the Tsarist regime; and others of the privileged class. It was these reactionaries who prompted the pogroms, incited the poor peasants, and brought in the gangs.

But under Denikin's rule, pogroms were a military activity. Then it was the military that initiated them and carried them out. Most of the local Christians had nothing to do with them. They were apathetic or hostile to Cossack atrocities. In some cases peasants from surrounding villages took part, but they did nothing more than take the plunder that the Cossacks were throwing away, or taking household goods from houses that the owners had been forced to abandon. Local residents rarely took part in pogroms. This occurred in Rossovo, Bohuslav, Fastiv; Boryspil.

Very seldom did local Christians actively participate or incite them, as in Boyarka and Rakitna (Kiev province). Rather we see local Christians treating Jews decently, hiding them in their homes, standing up for them, sending official delegations to the military commanders in the cities and various organizations, courageously and heroically risking their lives on their behalf, in Bila-Tserkava, Horodyshche, Hostomel, Veprik, Cherkasy (Kiev province); Borzna, Konotop, Niezhyn, Novy-Malyn; Boryspil; Dzhurin, Krivoye-Ozero (Podolia province); and in many other places. Many Jews owed their lives to that compassionate behavior, without which the devastation would have been much worse.

But the situation grew worse with time: the state of permanent pogrom was demoralizing. Robbery, murders, slaughters were perpetrated day or night, not just by criminals but by the regular army and its officers. It was done right in front of everyone, and the superior commanders either pretended not to know or gave tacit assent by not prohibiting it and by not punishing anyone. Pogroms were a legal way of life. Jewish possessions were for the taking, and gradually some of the local Christians joined in the robbery. In many cases Christian farmers, especially those in nearby villages, would not let Jews hide in their homes, supposedly because they were not permitted to do so. In the town of Kozyn (Kiev province) farmers hid Jews at first, but seeing the actions of the military authorities, they themselves beat the Jews. The same occurred in Stepantsi, and especially in Tagancha (Kiev province).

But the opposite also happened, and even where there was no moral repugnance at first, horrendous acts of violence elicited human compassion. For example in Niezhyn, where the Christian residents showed no sympathy towards the Jews, nevertheless, when they witnessed the horrors they hid Jews in their homes and sent a delegation led by priests to the military authorities to plead for the Jews. On those harrowing days some Christians showed great compassion by standing up for Jews at a time when just saying a good word about Jews was in itself a crime, and there were those who were beaten for doing that, in Borzna (Chernihiv province) and Horodyshche (Kiev province).

A most unusual case should be noted in Horodyshche concerning one Haritsai. Although he was a bandit who had taken part in an earlier pogrom there, he was grateful to Jews who had saved him from death at the hands of the Soviets, and he showed up at the last minute when Cossacks were about to shoot a group of Jews. He defended them so vigorously, with such moral conviction and devotion, that it even moved the Cossacks, and in that way he saved them from certain death.

In short, taking everything into consideration, the pogroms were simply a military tactic for the commanders of the Volunteer Army. In some cases state troopers (police) joined in. For example in Rossovo the police chief himself, along with his militia, shot Jews who had returned to the ruins of their homes after a pogrom. The militia did the same in Kokhnyn (Kiev province), police chief Pampushka in Stepanets, the militia in Stavishche (Kiev province), and elsewhere. By the way, the same Pampushka had been the leader of a partisan unit for the Bolsheviks. In general the police terrorized the Jews and extorted money from them. But the bulk of the pogroms were carried out by the regular Army. And by doing that it alienated itself even from the Christian population, even among the villagers, who were generally conservative, particularly in within the Pale of Settlement and who had looked upon the Volunteer Army as the liberators and "saviors"of Russia.

The Mass Rape of Women

The mass rape of Jewish women was the most distinctive, striking feature of the Volunteer Army pogroms. It put its special stamp on them. There had been horrendous slaughters before. One need only mention the slaughters of Petliura's Army in Proskurov and Felshtin in Feburary 1919; Grigoriev's bloodbaths in Cherkasy and Yelizavetgrad in May 1919. Rapes had been rare, few in number. But with the Volunteer Army it became systematic, along with plunder and murder. They raped women everywhere, even in the "quiet pogroms" and in the larger cities. In Yekaterinoslav they raped thousands of Jewish women. In smaller towns, it was hundreds which meanswomen, almost all those who could not manage to escape or hide themselves for long.

The manner in which it was done has already been noted. 1) It was done out in the open, in front of husbands, parents, and children. 2) No one was spared this horror for any reason or age, from little girls as young as 8 to elderly women. One might imagine that the reports from so many different local informers, as well as the special investigation on the rape of women, might be the nightmare of some delirium, but then one would have to draw the even more fantastic conclusion that hundreds of people who had never met each other had somehow colluded to make up the exact same story, using almost the very same words, even inventing the names of the victims. One would have to believe that masses of Jewish women went to doctors and midwives for help and, with no shame whatsoever, made up the foulest and vilest stories about themselves.

So horrendous are the accounts that they are difficult to grasp. Here are a few of the countless reports. In Korsun (Kiev province) two cases are documented of the rape of women in their seventies: In Rossovo a 75-year-old woman in Rossovo in front of her husband and daughters; in Tomashpil; and elsewhere. In Kremenchug six Cossacks raped a woman who was suffering from typhus. In Korsun they raped a woman who was on her deathbed, and she died on the spot. In Niezhyn and in Rossovo they raped women in childbed. In Pryluk they stopped a girl in the street in broad daylight across from the district office, they stripped her naked and raped her. Eight to ten Cossacks would rape one child. In Cherkasy they bit a raped girl from head to toe, till she was all swollen. In Borzna they seized a group of girls in the street, whipped them, then raped them.

They dragged Jewish women and girls out of their homes, and they never came back. Others were snatched straight out of trains. Many of the victims came down with the vilest venereal diseases. Others lost their sanity. They raped and then murdered many. Some women begged for death rather than be raped. And many Jews, old and young, ended up dead trying to protect their own from shame and tragedy. There are no words...

Humiliation and Torture

It would be hard to be original in cruelty after such pogrom criminals as those of Zelenyi's gangs and Sokolovsky's gangs, and Petliura's Atamans, Palienko (during the first pogrom in Zhitomir January 1919), [Ivan] Semosenko (the slaughter in Proskurov), and others.[26]

Yet in this respect the Volunteer Army managed to outdo them, both in the variety of violence and degradation and in the enthusiasm with which they committed them. First of all, there were methods

---

26   Almost 2,000 people were murdered in one day in Proskurov. See Peter Kenez, 'Pogroms and White Ideology in the Russian Civil War', in *Pogroms: Anti-Jewish Violence in Modern Russian History*, ed. by John D. Klier and Shlomo Lambroza (Cambridge: Cambridge University Press, 1992), pp. 293–313 (p. 295).

reminiscent of the Inquisition. These were the primary means to extort money from people, to ransom their freedom. Their methods were so varied, so thought-out and consistent, that it seemed as though they were not simple murderers doing their usual quick work, but rather serious, pious monks of the Inquisition attempting to extract the truth. Such techniques as threatening people with a rifle, putting them against a wall, beating them, brutalizing them, breaking their limbs — this was "banal," workaday.

The Volunteer Army employed "more refined" methods, for example hanging people to frighten them. This is how they did it. They would put a noose around the victim's neck and throw the rope over the first hook in the house, and they hanged him, not long enough to kill him — because they needed him alive to pay the ransom, or to show them where something was hidden — or just to watch him hanging there, between life and death. Then they let him down till he regained consciousness. Then they stuck a rifle into him, or hit him with a whip, and demanded that he show them what was hidden, that he give them money, etc. And they would do this until people brought the ransom money. There were cases where they hanged someone three times, Berkovich in Krivoye-Ozero; someone else seventeen times (Smilianski in Cherkasy, from whom they extorted half a million rubles); and a case where they compelled a high-school boy, Boris Zabarski in Fastiv, to put the rope around his father's neck.

They used medieval tortures using fire. They would burn someone's face with a candle, and they threw people into fires. In Bila-Tserkava, for example, they did it to a man named Grossman, who had escaped the pogrom in Volodarka, and he died. They would burn the hair on your head, the soles of your feet, etc. And they combined the tortures. They would hang someone and burn the soles of their feet with candles, as they did in Kaharlik. It was just like the Inquisition torture rack. They ripped the hair from your beard. They stuck needles into your feet, etc. In Boryspil they demanded 25,000 rubles from a man named Lilegart. First they knocked him to the ground and kicked him, then they threw him into a box and stabbed him with knives. Then they pulled him out, half-dead, and shot him right in front of his mother and sister.

The Volunteer Army murdered thousands of Jews, those gray-haired old "Communists" that they rounded up as they were studying *Gemara* in the prayer houses, those "Communist" infants in their cradles, along with their mothers and grandmothers. Among those murdered, the number of tortured elderly, women, and children is shocking. They shot people to death, but in greater numbers they stabbed them, slashed them with swords, chopped off their heads. Many died in homes that they set on fire, more than 100 in Fastiv alone, Lutshinets, Dzhurin, Yaruha (Podolia province). In Korsun they strangled 80-year-old Sukhodolski. They buried alive 90-year-old Frume Pekar in Rozhiv; two people in Tetiiv; Ben-Zion Evalenko in Obrukhov (but he got out alive), and more and more.

But such a death might have been preferable for those who were tortured endlessly, their tongues cut out (like Kisman in Fastiv, who had already been wounded by a bullet), their ears, their noses, their eyes gouged out (like Yampolski in Fastiv), their hands and feet cut off, etc. What can we say of the "idyllic scenes" staged by Russian officers? They strung Jews to sleighs instead of horses, as in Horodyshche. Or they ordered brutalized, half-naked people whose parents and children were murdered right in front of them to hold hands and merrily dance a *karahod* while singing, "Murder the Jews and save Russia!" in Mykhailivka (Kharkiv province); Kaharlik (Kiev province); Borzna (Chernihiv province); and elsewhere.

The Extermination of Jewish Communities

We have seen that the Volunteer Army was not satisfied with merely plundering Jewish possessions. They were just as inclined to simply destroy everything, and this annihilation was, so to speak, the ideal of the Volunteer Army: selflessly devoted to rooting out the Jews completely. We have already seen that the emptying out of household goods and furniture, and the burning down of homes and stores, was part of the plan, especially in the provinces of Kiev and Podolia. No other group had done this on such a massive scale, so systematically, or so thoroughly as the Volunteer Army. Many Jewish towns and villages had already suffered pogroms in 1919, but they had managed to hang on. The Volunteer Army now dealt them the death blow.

Other towns, like Fastiv, which had happily avoided the first wave of pogroms, and which had welcomed thousands of unfortunates who had fled from that hell, first experienced that kind of systematic annihilation at the hands of the Volunteer Army. Many towns were decimated by the burning down of houses: Bohuslav, Bila-Tserkava, Horodyshche, Hostomel, Korsun, Makarov, Rakitna, Rossovo, Talne, Shpola (Kiev province); Boryspil; Niezhyn; Krivoye-Ozero, Tomashpil, Myaskova, Savran (Podolia province), and others.

Towns like Fastiv, for example, with 10,000 Jewish residents, were left almost completely empty amidst the flames and smoke. In Fastiv alone, 200 Jewish houses were totally burned down, and as many shops. They systematically destroyed not only private property, but also community institutions. They demolished and burned Jewish prayer houses, hospitals, old-age homes, schools, free-loan associations, and cooperatives. In Bila-Tserkava they turned the *Talmud-Torah*[27] into an outhouse, and one part of its courtyard into a horse-stall, although there was a deserted horse shed nearby. They smashed the window panes and the oven doors. In Rossovo they destroyed the free-loan association. The Cossacks tore apart the drawers, the cabinets, the tables, the accounts. They broke into the warehouse and plundered everything. They struggled for a long time to break into the safe. Finally at one in the morning they put pyroxylin under the safe and blew up the whole building.

They destroyed Jewish homes and stores on a massive scale after first plundering them. One result of this was that economic life was paralyzed, because the terror and the attacks on Jews did not stop even in the "quiet pogroms." All this resulted in dozens of Jewish communities being annihilated. Life became unbearable in the towns and villages where there reigned a "permanent pogrom." So despite the fact that death lurked on the roads, the survivors fled wherever they could, starving, naked, barefoot, with the elderly and children. They would often stumble onto communities that had already been devastated. There these homeless would have to depend on charity.

As more and more villages were destroyed, and more people were made homeless, the availability of assistance dwindled. Many ended up horribly cramped in prayer houses and poorhouses, dying in huge numbers from hunger, cold, and even more from epidemics, especially typhus. The death rate among Jews at that time was so high that it was

---

27   Hebrew and Yiddish: traditional Jewish elementary school.

often impossible to bury them in the proper time, and corpses had to wait for graves. It can be said that if Jews were murdered by the thousands by Cossack bullets and swords, but they died by the tens of thousands in the suffering after the pogroms, from starvation, the cold, and typhus.

Indeed dozens of Jewish communities were rendered homeless: Boryspil, Boyarka, Hostomel, Dymer, Ignatovka, Yaruha, Kaharlik, Kobyzhcha, Kozyn, Krivoye-Ozero, Mironivka, Moshny, Orlovets, Pototsky, Rozhiv, Rosava, Tagancha, Tarashcha, Sharhorod, and others. Some of those who tried to return home were murdered, for example in Rosava, and at best they managed to escape again, as in Boyarka. The Cossacks burned down the ruined houses, or local peasants moved in. There was no going home.

But the ruined communities that could not manage to escape and had to remain were no better off. They, too, died by the thousands from the cold, starvation, typhus. The situation of such a well-established and solid community as Fastiv, after the first pogrom of September 22–26, 1919, is described in a report on relief assistance: "We evacuated 75 seriously wounded people to Kiev. A number of them were murdered in the hospital in Kiev during the pogrom there. We requisitioned 2 epidemics barracks for 500 people and two shared-living quarters. We are feeding 6,500 people in soup-kitchens. Ten to twenty people die every day." In such a small town as Vasilikov 400 Jews were sick with typhus in November 1919. In smaller towns, especially the more isolated ones, the situation was even worse.

The Volunteer Army did not devastate only Jewish communities in the towns, but also the tiny Jewish settlements in the villages. Their experienced eyes uncovered Jews everywhere. In the village of Gogolenko (Chernihiv province) there lived five Jewish families. They had been allowed to buy land for the first time after the Revolution, just like the farmers. The Cossacks destroyed everything, and they barely escaped with their lives to Borzna.

It was particularly painful to see Jewish farmers rooted out, along with so many other Jewish communities. Near Fastiv there were three Jewish agricultural colonies amidst a sea of farming villages. They were three Jewish islands of manual labor and the peaceful life of the plough: Koldubitskaya-Obraz-Tsovaya, Trilesy, and Tchervelenskaya. They had been granted the land even before Tsar Nikolai I. They had managed to prevent the Tsarist officials from taking their land for years. Three, four generations had worked the land. But the Volunteer Army destroyed them.

A special investigator described the devastation in the Koldubitskaya Colony. Petliura's Army committed the first pillaging when the Directorate escaped from Kiev, in February 1919. His gangs would not leave the Colony in peace all summer long. In August Petliura's units again came and left. They stole food and cattle, set fire to several homes, and murdered several people. Still, the Colony hung on. The Volunteer Army came at the beginning of September, and they continued to rob and beat people. When the Cossacks pulled out, they murdered a colonist who was digging potatoes in the garden.

During the battles between the Volunteer Army and the Bolsheviks outside Fastiv at the end of September, all the colonists, 200 souls, escaped to the village of Veprik, the district seat. Only the elderly stayed behind. A unit of the Volunteer Army soon entered Veprik, saw the Jews at the *skhod* (village square) and accused them of having joined the Bolsheviks, and of being spies. They began shooting them down. The *starshina*[28] and the *starosta*[29] were there, and they swore that the Jews had been with them the whole time, with the farmers.

Then they marched them under guard to Fastiv. On the road they robbed them, brutalized them, and seized all the girls. Two of them never returned. The Jews in Fastiv gave them a prayer-house, and these working people had to live off charity. Back in the Colony, the elderly had been murdered, some burned alive. The food, the cattle, and the horses had been stolen. The Colonists who were in Fastiv later recognized their horses pulling wagons for the officers. One officer offered to sell them back the horses as 10,000 rubles a piece. The other two colonies were annihilated in the same way.

Jewish farmers from the Rikun Colony (Dymer district, Kiev province) sent a letter to the supreme commander, General Dragomirov, protesting the fact that the Cossacks had stolen 10 cows, several horses, and all the poultry. Then they stole 60 head of cattle. They begged him to return their goods. The last lines of their complaint betray their deep anger as well as their naiveté: "If our horses and cows are not returned,

---

28   Ukrainian: village headman.
29   Ukrainian: district headman.

our Colony will come to an end, we will have to go back to the city or take up business."

The Officers

Let us note here another aspect of the Volunteer Army pogroms. On October 17–20, during the mass pogrom in Kiev, you could observe in Jewish homes the refined manners of uninvited guests who had been "well-educated," who spoke French, and even many musicians. These were officers of the Volunteer Army who had been members of the [Russian Imperial] Leib-Guard Preobrazhenska and Semyonov divisions and other regiments. They showed no "coarseness." In a firm, and in a manner-of-fact tone, they extorted money, jewelry, and gold. Sometimes one would politely request a handkerchief of fine cloth, saying he would return it clean. Not all the officers were so "refined," those commanders of the Ossetians, the Chechens, and other Caucasus tribes.

But when it came to committing pogroms, they were not inferior to their highborn comrades. On the contrary. As a general rule, the officers supported the troops under them, either openly or secretly. In Pryluk an officer of the Semyonov regiment saw a soldier in torn boots, and he said to him: "Why don't you go up to the first Jew and take his boots?" In Bila-Tserkava officer Yakovlev of the Second Terek Plastun Brigade[30] asked his commander, Colonel Shchepetilnikov, for clothes to dress in, and the reply was: "Rob a Jew. Nothing will happen." We have reports of officers plundering in Bogodukhov, Borzna, Boryspil, Horodyshche (Lieutenant Captain Svetsky and Ensign Kalgushkin); in Dymer (Lieutenant Colonel Beznebov), in Korsun, Kremenchug, Niezhyn, Pryluk, Fastiv, Cherkasy, Tomashpil, Yampol, Kurilovtsy, Tetiiv (Prince Golitsyn and Prince Lvov), and others.

In some places the officers initiated the pogroms: Boyarka, Rossovo, Krivoye-Ozero (Officer Mlashevsky), Mohilev-Podolsk (Colonel Mizernitsky), Miaskova, and others. Dr. S.,[31] on behalf of Dr. B., reports

---

30 Those infantry brigades were primarily formed by Kuban Cossacks.
31 This is undoubtedly Dr. Snisarenko who served in the Second Terek Plastun Brigade. The report dates from the time when the Volunteer Army was still strong in Ukraine [note by the author].

on pogroms led by officers in Bila-Tserkava: Ensign Kuzmichov recounts that Colonel Shchefetilnikov and other officers described how he had tortured a ten-year-old girl. He also told how his soldiers had raped women every day, and this account was gotten accurately straight from the Colonel.

Centurion Zhivodyarov, who has a lot of Jewish suffering on his conscience, stole a cow from a Jew and sold it for 22,000 "Nikolayev" rubles. Cavalry Capt. Kundo loaded onto his wagon six fox pelts, a gold watch, and other things that he had plundered from Jews. Capt. Podshivalov (of the 4th Company) took a piano in his wagon. Ensign Inzhuarov made it a specialty to rob doctors. He bragged to the above-mentioned Dr. B that he had made 400,000 rubles just from the dental instruments that he had plundered. Cornet Bandarenko would ride into town dressed as a civilian to facilitate his robberies. He told Dr. B. that wounded Jews should be killed, not treated. There were cases of plundering by officers whose cynicism was really unbelievable. In Cherkasy an officer of the Volunteer Army was quartered at the home of Israel Halpern. He was friendly to the family and would often eat with them. But as the Volunteer Army was retreating from Cherkasy, the very same officer plundered them completely, gun in hand. In Kremenchug a colonel even dragged away his host's furniture.

But the officers were not always enthusiastic plunderers. Sometimes they could be convinced to make a deal, and for a sum of money they would protect Jewish homes and shops from the pogrom. For the right bribe he would offer to protect the home and the shop from the pogrom. There were even whole groups of officers who did this. In Zolotonosha the Jews paid officers from the commander's guard 15,000 rubles per night, and they watched over many Jewish homes and stores. The same thing happened in Shpola. Officers were guarding there with one named Usov at the head. Similarly in Kiev, in Fastiv, and elsewhere.

"Contributions": Legal Robbery

Officers sometimes committed another kind of robbery, "legal" one could say. That was extortion, usually the privilege of the highest level of the Volunteer Army, the commanders and the garrison chiefs. Here is how they did it. While soldiers and lower officers "worked" the Jewish houses in a town, the commander or the garrison chief would send for the rabbi and the head of the community council and advised them "kindly" to bring a "gift" for the Volunteer Army. Sometimes he would be more honest and say that the Jews must pay such-and-such ransom money, to be paid within a day or two. There was some negotiating, and they would come to an understanding. That was how it was done in most cities. On December 22, 1919 (January 4, 1920) in Krivoye-Ozero, Dekonsky, the commander of the Volchanska Partisans, sent a written announcement, to this effect: "Inasmuch as the Jews have not helped the Volunteer Army at all, they have until the 24th to collect 200,000 rubles and 25 pairs of boots." He did not keep his word. On the 24th he took the money, but still launched a horrendous pogrom in which more than 600 people were murdered.

The worse the violence, the more Jews were willing to pay. And the more money the Volunteer Army earned from the activities of their commanders and garrison chiefs, the greater the ransom that was demanded. There was an instance in Lozovaya (Yekaterinoslav province) in which the commandant, in a great rage, first refused to hear of any "blood-stained Jewish money." But he soon let himself be talked into accepting the "gift" of 50,000 rubles. When enthusiasm grew for pogroms among the lower ranks, it was an opportunity for the higher-ups to demand "presents" a second and a third time for the Volunteer Army, which was shedding blood for the good of Russia (in Bobrovytsia, Borzna, Fastiv, from Rabbi Braslavsky, and elsewhere). The "contributions" were extortion money "so that no pogrom should take place" (in Vasilikov and elsewhere); or "so that the pogrom should be stopped" (for 200,000 in Pryluk); or "so that they should stop setting the fires" (for 500,000 in Talne); or "so that the killings should stop, but there's no guarantee against robbery" (Commandant Runtsev's words in Fastiv).

The Jews learned to fear the Volunteer Army and to give the required "gifts." But it was no protection against plunder and murder. The pogroms did not abate, nor did they end. They were given brutal warnings: "If not, then..." In Novy-Malyn, for example, even after the pogrom, the commander demanded 200,000 rubles. If not, then he would drown them all in the river.

Counter-espionage also took its share. In Pryluk, Palekha, the head of counter-espionage, demanded 250,000 rubles, in addition to the 200,000 that the commandant had extorted. If not, then there would be a pogrom. The militias, too, wanted their share. In Stepanets, Pampushka-Burlak, a well-known bandit whom the Volunteer Army had named chief of police, kept demanding "contributions." His deputy, Borbatenko, did likewise.

The Volunteer Army demanded not only money but clothes. In Konotop, for example, the commandant demanded 200 pairs of underwear. In Horodyshche they extorted 10,000 rubles worth of beef and chicken. The commander in Mykhailivka (Kharkiv province) surpassed all the others in his greed. He summoned Zelbet, the head of the Jewish community council, and ordered him to deliver 200,000 rubles in cash, a gold watch, two imported travel suitcases, two pairs of ladies' slippers size 39, two pairs of ladies' stockings, pepper, candles, tobacco, matches, etc. In addition, before he left town, he ordered Zelbet (as well as Limin and Vinitsky, who had already been plundered), to write a note certifying that the Volunteer Army had treated the Jews honorably, and that the Jews were happy with them.

You may well be asking yourself: Can all of this really be true about the officers of the Volunteer Army? Could it be really possible that there were not ten righteous men in this Sodom... honorable, upstanding, decent men who had joined the Army for idealistic reasons? If there were, then they should have upheld the honor and the very existence of the Army itself, and stood up for the Jews in their bleakest days of death and shame. But where were they?

It must be said that our people warmly hold in their hearts the memory of those who were decent and compassionate. We do not only remember the atrocities, but we create legends about our friends, about those who looked kindly on us. In almost every town we remember Christians who took the part of the Jews, those who hid them in their homes, and those who said a good word for us in those black days of calamity, and we bless them. But among these "righteous among the nations" you will rarely find the name of an officer. In Fastiv they tell of an officer named Ilyushin who protected several Jews (although some say he was paid for it). There is a report of three officers who warned the Jews in the village Gogolenko of the approach of soldier-criminals, and advised them to hide their best things. There is a story of an officer who tried to stop soldiers during the slaughter in Boyarka, and it is painfully recalled how he was insulted for it. There are very few instances. You can count them on your fingers.

During this entire period we did not hear of a single group of officers who protested against the pogroms. People are more apt to exaggerate the good and the honorable, than to point a finger. But if they remain silent, that means that aside from the few cases mentioned above, there is nothing to discuss. If there was indeed a group of officers who treated Jews better in their hearts, but not in the open, then they were silent, either out of fear or small-mindedness. They stood quietly to the side and let the overwhelming number of criminal officers lead the way, without protesting, without complaining, and their names will be dishonored and cursed for generations to come.

Self-Defense

Jews, especially the youth, have long realized that during the constant state of warfare in Ukraine, they could only count on themselves for their lives, their dignity, and their few possessions, and only with a rifle in hand. Furthermore, self-defense was a question of honor among the Jewish youth. Ukrainian Jews in self-defense sacrificed many lives, among them the youngest and the best. Which doesn't mean that it was effective.[32] All the regimes were helpless against the countryside, which was armed from head to toe. None of them succeeded in removing the weapons, however they might try. By contrast, it was very easy to disarm the cities, and that was what each regime did right away.

But Petliura's regime did seize the few weapons held by Jews. They constantly searched Jewish homes for weapons, an excuse, by the way, to rob and commit violent acts. Needless to say, after so many searches, Jews were left with very few weapons. Nevertheless, groups of Jewish youth managed to arm themselves, sometimes as part of the city guard, sometimes as Jewish self-defense groups. Such groups could fight back aginst a gang but were not in a position fend off a pogrom army, and most of them were killed, victims of their idealism and weakness.

---

32 The day on which the Volunteer Army entered Kiev, 18/31 August 1919, they murdered 37 Jewish youth who were members of the city guard, in the most brutal way. But it must be noted that Petliura's army had also entered Kiev, and retreated before the Volunteer Army a day later [note by the author].

There was no lack of provocation. In Horodyshche after the Soviets left on 3/16 August, a town guard was formed with 50 Jews and 20 Christians, which lasted several days. On 9/22 August a train transport of Cossacks arrived from Smila, headed by Lieutenant Captain Svetsky. A gang of 12 Cossacks entered the town and began plundering. An appeal was made to Svetsky, who was standing at the train station with the rest of the Cossacks, and he replied, "Those are not my Cossacks. Those are bandits in disguise." Then the town guard shot into the air and the "bandits" ran away. Two hours later Svetsky came into town to complain that they had shot at his Cossacks, and he demanded that they surrender their weapons. The guard hesitated, arguing that the countryside was full of gangs, and that as soon as the Volunteer Army left, there would certainly be a massacre. To which Svetsky gave "his word as a Russian officer" that no harm would come to the town. The guard surrendered 50 rifles, and immediately the Cossacks launched a pogrom that lasted 9 days.

In Korsun after the first pogrom (26/13 August) by the Volunteer Army, the authorities gave permission for Jews to organize a self-defense unit. In the middle of December, as the Volunteer Army began to retreat, the officer guard began to plunder. The Jewish self-defense unit drove them off and thing quieted down. Soon after that a unit of the Volchanska Partisans rode into town. They disarmed the self-defense unit, and then proceeded to launch a pogrom unimpeded.

Incidentally, in those places where Jewish youth had somehow miraculously held on to their weapons, a strong resistance was put up against the soldier-criminals. In Steblev (Kiev province) the Jewish self-defense fought the Cossacks, and narrowly drove them out of town. Later they fought off an attack by 400 criminals under Ataman Tuz, and in the process took 3 machine guns, rifles, ammunition, etc. When the Volunteer Army was retreating from the area, the self-defense protected the town, and stopped them from entering.

IV. The Causes of the Pogroms.
Pogroms as Part of the Military and Political Program. The Connection to the High Command

We have seen that pogroms were the rule, not the exception, for the Volunteer Army. They were a constant during their entire quest, from its first speedy victories to its shameful defeat. It was an essential element of their style of warfare. Where, then, did that come from? What were the deep motives that drove a large army to plunder and slaughter, indeed an army that was going to "save Russia" and establish "law and order," and which, furthermore, was led by veteran, experienced generals, exemplars of military discipline? What was its connection to the methods of war, its requirements, or its objective?

Opportunities for Pogroms

First, what were the opportunities? The conditions were longstanding, psychological, with deep roots. By contrast, the opportunities were just a detail, the accident of chance in a given place at a given time, for example, the relations between the Jews and the Volunteer Army, the local history, the disputes, etc. — any of which might lead them to commit a pogrom in a particular place. If we pay close attention to the way in which pogroms occurred and how they developed, it becomes clear that in the overwhelming majority of cases there was no obvious trigger for the pogrom. We must note again that they occurred as soon as military units entered a town, before there were any relations with the Jewish community and any possible conflict. Furthermore, in many instances the pogrom started with the Jewish delegation that came to welcome the Volunteer Army with bread and salt.

In some cases the blame was placed on rumors that were spread — as a provocation — that the Jews had shot at the Volunteer Army. Those were instances when the Army had to retreat before the Reds for a few days (sometimes for just a few hours, as in Korsun, for example), and then returned to take the town. This occurred in Borzna, Niezhyn, Novy-Malyn, Fastiv, Kiev, and elsewhere. No less than a Volunteer Army commander reported, in an official communication, that Jews had shot at the Army when it was retreating from Novy-Malyn. And he said, by the way, that "measures had been taken" against them. It is not difficult to guess what he meant by that.

Osvag, the official propaganda organ, had no qualms about spreading this story of "Jewish shooting" in Kiev on October 14/19, when a small Bolshevik military unit of the Irpen detachment broke through and there was fighting in the streets. But even if this story about "Jewish shooting" in a few places had been true, would that have justified pogroms in all of Ukraine, where there were no such reports? Not only that, but there are facts, and even a report of a special investigation, that totally demolish the entire myth of Jewish shooting. On the days of the terrible Kiev pogrom, on 17–20 of October 1919, an official Kiev newspaper, *Vecherniye Ogni*, reported, in a series of issues (No. 38, 39, and 40) carried the story of the "Jewish shooting." But a number of centrist, and even conservative organizations (the Union for the Regeneration of Russia, the National Center, the National Union, the Teachers' Union, the City Association, and others) researched the "facts" in that report, and concluded that they had been completely fabricated, and not very well at that. Let us consider one of those "facts," No. 13. The newspaper said this: "On 3/16 October, four Jews and one Christian shot from the roof at No. 18 Kreshchatik Street. They were brought down from the roof and shot." Here is what the investigators reported: "The house at No. 18 Kreshchatik Street is the Kiev City Hall. The press office of the City Hall sent a letter to the editor of *Vecherniye Ogni*. It is evident from that letter that after 2/15 October Volchanska Partisans[33] occupied the City Hall and hung the Russian National flag from the balcony. And that same day they already had a mess hall organized in the City Hall. Therefore it is totally out of the question that people were shooting from the roof on 3/16." The investigators rejected all the other "facts" with the same kind of proof.

This refutation was posted in Kiev on all the light-poles, but *Vecherniye Ogni* did not apologize. Furthermore, General Dragomirov appointed a

---

33   This was a military unit infamous for its pogrom massacres in Korsun, Fastiv, and other towns [note by the author].

special commission headed by Senator Guliayev to again investigate the matter, and that commission, too, found absolutely nothing to confirm the story of "Jewish shooting." And not out of love for the Jews.

The myth of shootings in Novy-Malyn was no more believable. About 70 Jewish families lived there among Christians. During the fighting between the Volunteer Army and the Bolsheviks for that town, there was heavy firing of artillery and machine guns. Jews and Christians would hide in the cellars of each others' houses. During the last volleys, just before the Volunteer Army took over the city, Jews went to hide with Christians, because at that time the shooting was in the Jewish part of town, which lies along the Dniester River. The Bolsheviks, who still held the town, went into the abandoned Jewish homes and fired from there. A delegation of Christians later went to the commander of the Volunteer Army and attested that the Jews had had nothing to do with the shooting.

There was even a special "certification" from their Christian neighbors on 2/15 October, which they gave to the Jews, which stated: "We, the undersigned residents of Novy-Malyn, attest that what was written in *Kievlyanin* No. 21, 14/27 November, is not true. The Jews in town did no harm to the Volunteer Army and did not shoot at them." They also confirmed that relations were good between Jews and Christians, and that Jews had not been active in Soviet institutions. The certification was signed by homeowner Grigory Ivanovich Filipenko; postmaster Yushchenko; Aleksander and Peter Khonak; a teacher, Yelisina; and others, including several councilmen from the City Hall. The mayor confirmed the signatures.

It was the same with the "shootings" in Fastiv and elsewhere. Furthermore, there is evidence that in all these cases the pogrom had been organized in advance, secretly planned even before the beginning of the war. Residents of Kiev, both Christians and Jews, who had fled the city on October 14th with the Volunteer Army before the advancing Bolsheviks report that in Darnitsa, the nearest village, they heard nonstop agitation for a pogrom in Kiev. That was before any talk of "Jewish shooting," and before anyone had been "taken from the roof with machine guns."

There are likewise reports about Fastiv during the days when the Volunteer Army was still retreating before the Bolsheviks to the nearest village, Kozhanka. They report, in the name of Dr. Snisarenko, who retreated with the Second Terek Plastun Brigade, that the commander of the brigade, Belogortsev, had promised to "hand over Fastiv" to the Cossacks, who would take the town.

It is clear. The fabrications about "Jewish shooting" or that that they cried "Hurrah" in honor of the oncoming Bolsheviks, as in Fastiv, were nothing more than pretexts. It is evident that in all these towns the pogroms had actually started before the Volunteer Army was forced to retreat, in fact as soon as it had entered the town. And that was how they occurred everywhere. The slaughter only worsened after the myths about the shootings were spread.

The stories are all the more suspect when they are repeated after the pogrom not by the Army that committed it, but by those who feel the need to defend them, for they understand what a terrible impression it makes on the larger world at a time when the civil war is complicated by international interests. If they wish to excuse a pogrom with the myth of "Jewish shooting," then they have answer the question, what came first, the myth or the pogrom? Who is it that needs the pretext? Do the Cossacks need it, when they drive in with their wagons and signs reading, "Murder the Jews and Save Russia?" This is clear: Chance is not important. What is important is that it is always easier to perpetrate a pogrom where there is already an established tradition. The causes run much deeper.

The Volunteer Army

The Volunteer Army consisted mostly of volunteers, partisans. They tried a draft, but the population would not go along and little came of it. The two main features of the Army were an abundance of officers who had fled Soviet Russia, and far too many Cossacks, especially Asian horsemen of various savage tribes: Chechens, Ossetians, etc. K. N. Sokolov, a member of Denikin's dictatorship and a minister in his regime, who recently published a book, *The Regime of General Denikin* (Sofia, 1921), writes about the Army: "We were in a bad way. Our military strength lay in the Kuban Cossacks who were under the demagogic influence of the plague of Black Hundred Ukrainian nationalists (supporters of Cossack Ukrainian separatism). The Russians gave us Bolsheviks, half-Leninist youth, or moderate supporters of 'Revolutionary Democracy.' We relied militarily on the Cossacks. It was not for nothing that General

Denikin had written in August 1918 to the Kuban Ataman, 'It is certain that only the Cossack and mountain (Caucasus) people have the right to rule themselves, because they have resisted their enemies and their murderers.'" (p. 57)

These were the wild Cossacks and tribes of the Caucasus. Their officers were so numerous in the Volunteer Army that they comprised entire military units, and their generals headed companies. V. V. Shulgin, editor of *Kievlyanin*, an insider and a superbly informed man, recounts enthusiastically that when the Volunteer Army was passing through Kiev on October 14/19, no less than supreme commander General Dragomirov stopped soldiers and cadets who were deserting on the suspension bridge and ordered them to return to the battle against the Bolsheviks.

We have an authoritative reading of the situation with the Army — its officers, and the half-wild tribes — at the time when they penetrated deep into Ukraine, from its commander-in-chief, General Denikin himself. On July 26 (August 8) 1919, at 2 o'clock there came a Jewish delegation to see him at Rostov-on-Don. Among the delegation were representatives of these communities: M. S. Bruk from Yekaterinoslav; Dr. L. B. Vilensky from Kharkiv; Dr. Z. Goldenberg from Rostov; Dr. A. I. Yevinson from Taganrog. The delegation had come to complain of the violence that the Cossacks were perpetrating in the Kharkiv and Yekaterinoslav provinces. To which General Denikin responded: "Yes, no good at all can come from people of such low character. These aren't the people who joined the Volunteer Army for an ideal, these are just dregs."[34]

But if it was neither ideals nor compulsion, then what drove "people of such low character" to attempt such a risky endeavor as "to save Russia?" Was it high wages, perhaps, or good working conditions? Certainly not! K. N. Sokolov, who is supremely well-informed about this, explains the upkeep of the Army: "We always maintained the Army poorly. We paid it poorly and clothed them poorly. Leaders at the front received exactly the same paltry change as the officials in the rear. But since the Army was on the move, and, furthermore, there was a shortage of paper currency, they often received no pay at all. When it came to

---

34 The Jewish delegation recorded this conversation with General Denikin and sent it straight to the Editorial Board along with other documents on the pogrom in the Kharkiv community. To my knowledge it has not been published before [note by the author].

clothing, that was also terrible... By the Fall (of 1919) it was already obvious that the Army would freeze in the Winter" (p. 192). We hear the same from another source, no less authoritative on this matter, and who was closely tied to the Volunteer Army, with its supreme commanders, and its political leaders. We are referring to V. V. Shulgin's article "Two Armies" in *Kievlyanin* No. 67, 13/26 November. Shulgin compares the Bolsheviks and the Volunteer Army. When he writes about the Volunteer Army he pretends to be neutral, but it is clear that he is quite bitter.

V. Shulgin would have us believe that "the aim of the Volunteer Army is — to protect and save the peaceful working people from the awful rule of do-nothings who took power by the gun." From which he concludes: "In that case, the Volunteer Army would necessarily have disintegrated if it had to depend on plunder for its livelihood." The prophetic accuracy of this observation becomes even clearer, when Shulgin explains the source of this "livelihood:" "Of course, it would not have occurred to anyone to plunder if the Army had gotten everything that it deserved, if it didn't have to freeze and starve. Just ask, and you will hear the plain truth, that the tradition of plunder grows largely out of bitter needs."

K. N. Sokolov writes more frankly about the "livelihood" of the Volunteer Army: "Moving back away from the front line, anyone who could do so would take care of business by making money dishonestly. On the front things were even simpler. "Appropriated Property"[35] (appropriating what the soldiers had plundered) became integral to the way of life of our Army at a time when plundered property was its main source — if not its only source — of livelihood.

But in addition to this kind of "Appropriated Property," which was considered lawful, and for which an account had to be given, another kind of "Appropriated Property" developed: plain robbery, committed by individuals and groups. We would hear reports, usually far from the front, of individuals and military units amassing huge quantities of goods. Once in Rostov in the winter, we saw a popular military leader traveling on a train to get some rest with his young officers. It was a gigantic train with dozens of cars loaded with merchandise, sugar, and

---

35 'Realdov' in Russian, an abbreviation for 'voenno realzatsiia dobychi', meaning appropriating what the military has seized from the enemy [note by the author].

all kinds of other things. The tracks of the Rostov train station were busy with it for quite a while." (pp. 193–94)

Shulgin sees the solution to those "bitter needs" this way: "It is better to have a smaller army, well equipped with everything that it needs, than a larger army that depends on its livelihood in the manner of Wallenstein, from plunder."[36] Because, predicts Shulgin, "such an army will not last for long." So we have it from the highest authorities, the most devoted friends of the Volunteer Army, that two of its prominent features were: 1. It is "people of low character" who joined it, not motivated by ideals (and not mobilized against their will). 2) This was an army that equipped itself "in the manner of Wallenstein," meaning by plundering. This helps us understand why the Volunteer Army attracted a lowly element who were often nothing more than bandits like I. T. Struk, for example.

It is worth exploring the career of this fine young man in the Volunteer Army. Ilya Timofeyevich Struk, a peasant from the village of Griny in the Hornostapol district of the Kiev province, went to a village school and began his military career in 1917, during the period of the Central Rada. He organized a unit of the *Vil'na Kozatstvo*,[37] that is to say of the Ukrainian National Army. He was no longer needed during the period of the Hetman under the German occupation (March–November 1918), so he turned to speculation and counterfeiting, and the police were looking for him.

When the Ukrainian Directorate revolted against the Hetmanate (November–December 1918) he formed a military partisan unit, extorted "contributions," and openly robbed Jews in the Hornostapol-Chernobyl region. Incidentally, he murdered a postal service official in the town of Malyn at the beginning of January 1919. The Malyn commandant arrested Struk and sent him off to Kiev, and there he was released. The Bolsheviks were then starting to fight against the Directorate. Struk sided with the Bolsheviks and published a Bolshevik manifesto aimed at the peasants.

He was sent to the front with his unit, and there, in his first battle, he betrayed the Bolsheviks and again sided with the Ukrainians. From

---

36 Albrecht von Wallenstein organized mercenary troops for Emperor Ferdinand II during the Thirty Years' War.

37 Russian: Free Cossacks, Ukrainian nationalist militia.

then on he and his men repeatedly committed pogroms for 9 months in Hornostapol, Chernobyl, and elsewhere, with this slogan: "Murder Jews! Save Soviet power without communes!" Then the Volunteer Army took Kiev.

For General Bredov, military chief of the Volunteer Army in the Kiev region, it was no obstacle to welcome this criminal into the Army. They asked Struk to organize "the first Little Russia partisan military unit," and crowned him Colonel in September 1919.[38] General Bredov knew perfectly well who Struk was. He received a written report on him from a Christian, Melnichenko, who knew Struk extremely well. In addition, he was informed by Professor Odinets, who was chairman of the regional committee of the Union for the Regeneration of Russia, and who possessed all the materials concerning Struk's atrocities, including his published pogrom proclamations. Struk's new allies did not interfere with his usual pogrom activities. For an entire winter, he and his gang — now in the guise of Russian patriots — terrorized the Jewish residents of Podol (Kiev province) and extorted "contributions" again and again. When the Volunteer Army retreats from Kiev, we find Struk in Odessa, where he continues to terrorize and plunder Jews. He called this a "peasant military unit" of the Volunteer Army in January 1920.[39]

Now we can begin to understand the kernel of truth when Cossacks and Chechens — those saviors of Russia — say that they were "permitted to go wild for three days." Such an army required some compensation if they were to obey orders and go into battle. What better compensation could they be given than to give them free reign over populated towns, or at least some people? We have already noted that when Belogortsev, commander of the Second Terek Plastun Brigade, wanted to motivate his Cossacks to "liberate" Fastiv, he "handed them the town." A Jewish delegation in Kremenchug, one of many like it, which came to plead to stop a pogrom, told the commander that the military leaders had let the Cossacks go wild for three days. The commander in Horodyshche said the same: We let the Cossacks go wild for 48 hours, "for our purposes." And the same was reported of other commanders and garrison chiefs.

---

38 See the newspaper *Kievskaya Rus*, No. 5, 25 November 1919 [note by the author].
39 Struk's proclamation on this was published in the newspaper *Odeski Listak*, No. 14, 15/28 January 1920 [note by the author].

Shulgin was right on both counts, both when he valued the Volunteer Army for taking care of its own needs and when he predicted its failure. His prophesy came true, that such an army would not last long, and it failed much sooner than he had thought. It became evident right in the pogroms. The lack of discipline went so far that when two soldiers of the Ismailov regiment began to strip Jews in Pryluk in the street in the middle of the day, and an officer ordered them to let the Jews go, one of the soldiers shot the officer. There were similar reports from Bila-Tserkava, Boyarka, and elsewhere.

We will see later why, when a town was handed over to the Cossacks, the Jews were being targeted. But even what we have already noted is sufficient to come to one conclusion: If in Novy-Malyn the Cossacks say that they were "permitted to go wild for three days," then that is a much more frank, accurate, and convincing explanation for the pogrom than to say that it was because Jews had been shooting at the Army.

We have already noted two prominent aspects of the Volunteer Army: the "dregs" and its livelihood "in the manner of Wallenstein," which is to say by plundering. That was the economic need underlying of their pogroms. But an ideology was also necessary, because that economic need, if unchecked, might go too far. "After plundering the Jewish population, they started to rob Russians, too," complained Colonel Sakharov, garrison chief in Bila-Tserkava, in his order number 10 of 1/14 October. That is why he commanded them to stop the pogrom. It was too dangerous to allow it free rein, without restraint or regulation. For its own survival, the Army had to take control of its "bitter needs" by limiting it in a specific way. It dawned on them that with certain regulations the "bitter needs" could be exploited for the military objective of the Volunteer Army, which was the war against Bolshevism.

They needed an ideology that would link "Beat the Jews!" to "Save Russia!" — meaning the struggle against the Bolsheviks. It was not necessary to look hard for such an ideology or to dream one up. It was easy to find, already fully formed, in the old Tsarist regime, especially in its attitude towards Jews during the World War. Who didn't already know that the Jews were the enemies of Russia, that the Jews had betrayed the Russian Army, etc.?

To our knowledge the first indication of this ideology of the Volunteer Army dates from the end of November 1918, when the Army was just starting to be organized. They were just getting ready for the actual war, and in the meantime it was not actually campaigning for Russia, but for recognition of themselves and sympathy from those who sought someone to "save" Russia. First of all they needed to make clear to them what a victory of the Volunteer Army would mean, and secondly, who the enemies of Russia were against whom they were waging war. Apparently that was the purpose of the proclamation, "A Call to the Russian People from the Army of the South,"[40] signed by "the Army of the South," 24 November (7 December) 1918, Rostov-on-Don. That appeal starts with the second point: the enemy. Here it explains at length "what Socialism and Bolshevism have done to the people." It says that "Russia has failed the Allies. Everything is ruined, destroyed," etc. And who is to blame? Here is the answer: "They, the kikes — Bronstein (Trotsky), Nakhamkes (Steklov), Tsederboym (Martov), Goldman (Gorev), Kirbis (Kerensky), Lieberman (Chernov) — have no interest in Russia or in Russia's welfare. They dream and strive to ruin Russia and to render the Russian people helpless before their sworn enemies and plunderers."

The proclamation repeatedly stresses the unique ability of the Jews to devastate Russia: "In order to better deceive the people (the Russians)," says the proclamation, "they have even changed their names: Layb Bronstein took the family name Trotsky, Lieberman took the name Chernov, Kirbis calls himself Kerensky," etc. "In addition to material ruination, they, the Bronshayns, the Nakhamkes, and others, have debased the spirit of the people." These "kikes" have "swindled" the people and conspired to bring about complete ruination and destruction, etc. In addition, they have incited the people to "beat the priests and throw out holy images (icons)." And instead of one Tsar, they have installed many little emperors, some of them Jews, to boot." That was point 2: the enemy.

Point 1, the purpose, is explained this way: "They (the kikes) say that robbing the landowners and ruining them is the same as if they ruined themselves. First of all, our landowners are our own, Russians, members of the Russian people. Secondly, they worked the land better, gave the people and the government better food, better cattle, better produce... They say, 'Let's divide up the land (of the landowners), but they don't

---

40   Russian: *Golos k Russkomu narodu ot Iuzhnoi Armii.*

say how much land each person could get. And there is really very little privately-owned land — and none at all in many places — which means that there is nothing to divide up..." The "Army of the South" appeals wholeheartedly to the Russian Orthodox people: "Stop selling your souls to the kikes! Throw off the yoke of the kikes."

So we can summarize the program of the "Army of the South" this way: 1. Its purpose: the lands of the landowners may not be touched because a) they are "our own people" and b) they have nothing to be taken ("they have little land"). 2. Its enemy: the "kikes" and only the "kikes," Chernov and the others, whom the world takes for Russians but who are really "kikes" in disguise. The "kikes" strive to destroy Russia, and they tear down the Orthodox Church. 3. Its means: throw off the yoke of the "kikes."

But they were not very strict about their program, and they played down parts of it in certain regions, especially the part about the property of the landowners. In the Don and Kuban region, in the southern steppes, where the peasants have plenty of land, they could say what they dared not say in Ukraine, where the vast majority of peasants had no land, particularly after the Soviet regime took the land away from the landowners, and the peasants would not give it back. The generals understood this, and we see, indeed, that they talked much less in Ukraine about privately-held land, and they even told them to appease that hunger for land.

On the subject of agrarian reform and other social and political programs, the Volunteer Army reflected the views of those who wished to restore the Tsarist monarchy and return to the "old regime" — that was evident in many ways. But within the bounds of our present work at hand we must limit ourselves to the essentials. The best witness for the social and political plans of the Volunteer Army is certainly the much-quoted K. N. Sokolov, one of the creators of those plans. He certainly would not wish to besmirch those plans. This is what he says in his book, *General Denikin's Government*: "We wished to address the question of land properly, honestly, with justice and fairness. On 24 March 1919, General Denikin wrote in his memo on the question of land that first of all, 'THE OWNERS RETAIN THE RIGHT TO THEIR LAND. THAT MEANS THAT WE WILL RETURN TO THE LANDOWNERS WHAT IS THEIRS BY RIGHT.'" (emphasis by N. Shtif)

K. N. Sokolov himself did not agree with that plan: "We may consider the seizure of that land 'immoral,' but it must be legalized, because it is 'politically necessary.'" Sokolov interprets Denikin's plan in such a way as to turn it into a legal maneuver: "To placate the rights of the aggrieved, the landowners may make a claim to be compensated for the land that was seized." This was indeed a fine interpretation, but he admits that "in practice, they returned the land to the landowners by force (p. 287). There were terrible instances when we supported the landowners and routed the peasants (p. 187). But a little further on, we hear, not about "terrible instances," but about a government program. "At the end of June 1919 (when the Army began to move quickly deep into Ukraine) regulations were issued concerning grass land. The government promised half the crop to the owners and half to the peasants, and as for compensation, the peasants would get two thirds and the owners one third, etc. (p. 188)

That was how they dealt with agrarian reform "properly and with fairness." It was even worse when it came to the issue of labor. Sokolov himself admitted that it was a lost cause: "The labor issue for us was fundamentally lost. We could not make the workers happy… simply because we could not regulate life… furthermore we were counting on the peasants, not the workers" (p. 186). And we have already seen how they satisfied the peasants.

Finally, on the national question. K. N. Sokolov, who was considered radical on the land issue by his fellow ministers, was rigid on this issue: "With whom have we been constantly and openly at odds? The Ukrainian political groups of the Samostina-Petliura stripe."[41] One might think that they had tried to reach an agreement with other, more moderate Ukrainian political groups. But Sokolov leaves no room for doubt. He often says, "With our overly-rigid political stand on the question of Ukraine, we repelled even the moderate circles of Ukrainian society that supported a federation with Russia" (p. 283). Now everyone knows exactly what their political stand was. They carved Ukraine into three separate regions (Kiev, Kharkiv, and New Russia), and they gave it to "the government" of General Dragomirov and his mentor, V. Shulgin, that Ukraine-hater. Right in the very first issue of *Kievlyanin* Shulgin explained: "Yes, this region is Russian… We

---

41   The Ukrainian independence movement.

will not cede it to the Ukrainian traitors who have ruined it, and not to the Jewish hangmen who have drenched it in blood" in *Kievlyanin* No. 1, 21 August/3 September 1919. They even expunged the name "Ukraine," which they once again referred to as "Little Russia." In his appeal to the "Little Russians," General Denikin promised them "a unified, indivisible Russia" and a Tsarist Russian school. The "Little Russians" could also have schools in their mother tongue, if they wished... supported by private means. In short, they were throwing Ukraine back into the days of Nikolai I, before education minister Count Ignatiev.

Sokolov emphasizes the last part, and summing up, admits bitterly: "It was not easy... The intelligentsia did not trust us. The workers hated us. The peasants suspected us" (p. 168). For him to say "suspected" is an understatement. They revolted against the Volunteer Army with weapons. As the Army retreated, the peasants supported the Bolsheviks, Petliura, and other Atamans against the Army. It was above all the anarchist bandit Makhno who attracted them, and who roamed over all of our supreme commander Denikin's territory, invading Yekaterinoslav, and taking over the most important train junctions, etc." (p. 190)

That was the social and political program at the highest level, where political decisions were made. But for most of the officers, even that program was too "left," too "Kadet." There developed "a political rift between him — Denikin — and the officers of the Volunteer Army... General Denikin turned out "too leftist" for his army." (p. 195) K. N. Sokolov qualifies this. He explains that "it would be unfair to consider the masses of officers 'reactionaries' or landowners themselves." But he must admit that the "gradualist liberalism" which was permitted to grow, and partially approved, in Rostov and in Taganrog, was alien to the most activist (officers)" (p. 195). He is referring here to liberalism "for export."[42]

Both sides agreed on one thing: K. N. Sokolov says openly that "the masses of people, including the military, were infused with

---

42 K. N. Sokolov often says that 'liberalism', and specifically the liberal declaration of March 1919 on the aims of the Volunteer Army, was 'made for export' (p. 123). 'The representatives of the Entente at Headquarters made it clear to the High Command that we needed to have a liberal declaration to allay any suspicions concerning our reactionary aims' [note by the author].

anti-Semitism." (pp. 103–04) The plan concerning the "kikes" was of prime importance to the Volunteer Army, considering such an ideology and such a program. Since its program was so full of omissions, the "kikes" could serve to fill in whenever agitation was needed.

Pogrom Agitation

As soon as the Volunteer Army entered a town, orders against "the kike-commissars" would appear on the walls. The officers, like Count Urusov in Bobrovytsia, made speeches against the Jews at peasant gatherings (*skhod*) and elsewhere. They agitated against "the kikes" at full blast. The higher echelons were no better than the lower. In Kiev province, for example, they issued a "mobilization appeal to the peasants" in which they explained all about Bolshevism: "Now what kind of person was the Bolshevik leader Trotsky originally, if not the elegant Layb Bronstein, whom no respectable person would ever have permitted into his home? And now he is an extremely important person, and sits in Moscow instead of the Tsar!" (*To the Peasants on Mobilization*, 25 October/7 November 1919).

That appeal was also posted in Kiev, and was published in *Kievlyanin* and in the semi-official *Narodnaya Gazeta*. In official war communiqués the command accused the Jews of shooting at the Volunteer Army, which had caused their defeats (as in Novy-Malyn). And they alleged that Jews made up a large part of the Red Army, and fought the fiercest against the Volunteer Army.

General Bredov did the same, spreading the myth of "Jewish shooting" in a more subtle, disguised way. And he did it at the very worst time for the Jews of Kiev, the tragic days of 14/19 October 1919. There was indeed fighting with a small Bolshevik military unit in the streets of Kiev. There was constant incitement against the Jews. They were preparing a pogrom, and to that end they spread the rumor that Jews had fired on the Volunteer Army. On 17/18 October the Volunteer Army was victorious, and they launched a horrendous pogrom. At such a juncture, General Bredov issued an order that seemed to call for an end to it (5/18 October). But just what was in that order? This is how he calmed down the agitated Volunteer Army: "Volunteers! Be bold against the enemy, as well as the peaceful residents and the defeated enemy: that will be to your credit." It is not hard to discern who the "defeated enemy" was in Kiev.

Mamontov, another prominent general, speaks more plainly, more coarsely. In September 1919, in his proclamation to the residents of the towns of Kozlov, Tambov, and Yelets, he said to the peasants: "Arm yourselves and rise up against our common enemy on Russian soil, the Jew — the Bolshevik — the Communist. Soon we will breathe free, free of the yoke of the Devil, which has enslaved us in shackles, destroyed our faith, our church... May we crush the power of the Devil that thrives in the hearts of the Judeo-Communists."[43]

Two themes were prominent in pogrom agitation: the persecution of the Orthodox Church and the *Cherezvichayka*.[44] The "persecution" was cleverly fabricated to tap into the religious fanaticism of the ignorant masses, peasants and townspeople. We have already seen how General Mamontov did this. The prominent colonel, Struk, followed his example, when he said in his proclamation: "They close the churches, they tear down our holy icons" (Odessa, January 1920). "All the saints call on you in the ranks to force the Devil's tribe (There is no doubt about this reference — N. S.) to allow Christians to live and believe freely" (Kiev, November 1919).

The *Cherezvichayka*, which was thoroughly hated by the people, was also blamed on the Jews. That was the surest way to inflame bloodthirsty impulses, second only to the persecution of the church, even among educated circles. Harrowing scenes played out in Kiev in the first days of the Volunteer Army. All someone had to do was to yell, "There he is, an agent of the *Cherezvichayka!*" and people would attack a person on the street and tear him to pieces. There were many victims who were murdered in the same way. Orders against such savagery were issued for world opinion. But in the meantime they were digging up buried corpses, and opening up hidden cellars — real and imagined — to show the world the atrocities of the *Cheka*. And they did this constantly blaming the Jews.

---

43   This proclamation was published by Col. Malone, Member of the English Parliament, in his book *The Russian Republic*. Our text is translated from the English [note by the author].

44   *Cheka* is an acronym of the Russian words 'Extraordinary Commission' for Combatting Counterrevolution, Speculation, etc. It was the secret political police of the Soviet Union.

We have already noted that in his very first article in the new *Kievlyanin*, Shulgin had already identified the Jews as the *Cheka*, "The Jewish hangmen who have drenched (our country) in blood." The "Jewish *Cheka*" was the most common theme in *Kievlyanin* and in pogrom agitation in general: "Trotsky is still running around on all the fronts, encouraging the bloody work of the Jewish *Cherezvichayka*" (Shulgin, in *Kievlyanin* No. 7, 10/28 September 1919). "The Trotskys, the Nakhamkes, the Rafes are waging war for equal rights, but they sentence people to death just because they are Russians." ([Anatolii Invanovich] Savenko, in *Kievlyanin* No. 1, 21 August/3 September 1919); etc.

There was no lack of other propaganda for pogrom agitation in the Volunteer Army. They even blamed pogroms on the "kike-communists" themselves: Jews perpetrated pogroms on themselves so as to be able to put the blame them on the Volunteer Army and discredit it. So said the commander in Niezhyn, when he reported that "the plundering and the savagery was mostly committed by the Trotsky-Bronsteins, the Nakhamkes, and the other mercenaries" (Order no. 11, dated 12/25 September 1919).

In addition to the military command, other official institutions incited pogroms, the *Osvag*[45] the semi-official press, individuals, and religious leaders. On July 26 (August 8) 1919, a Jewish delegation had already complained to General Denikin about the anti-Semitic agitation by the *Osvag*. They brought him such leaflets with titled, *Workers, Red Army*, and *Everyone, Everyone*. In the middle of Ukraine, in Kiev, they named as head of the *Osvag* the infamous Jew-hater Savenko who had been prominent in the Beilis trial.[46]

If we wish to grasp what *Osvag* was, we can rely again on K. N. Sokolov. He was the head of *Osvag*, its leader. Sokolov recounts "with pride and joy" that some famous artists, scholars, and writers worked for *Osvag*, among them E. Grimm, the former rector of the University of Petersburg; and B. Engelgardt, former Deputy in the Duma and commander of the Tavrichesky[47] Palace during the first days of the

---

45 Abbreviation of the Russian Osvedomitel'noe Agenstvo [Information Agency], the official propaganda organ of the Volunteer Army. It was later called the Otdel' Propagandy [Propaganda Department].

46 Menakhem Mendel Beilis was a Ukrainian Jew who was falsely accused of ritual murder in 1913.

47 Tauride.

Revolution. But he admits that "we had in the provinces (in Osvag) mostly ignorant good-for-nothings and careerist parasites. There were people lacking in conscience, prone to criminality." (p. 105) He says very guardedly that the naming of Savenko as chief of Osvag in Kiev "caused a great uproar and was objected to on many grounds." (p. 174)

We can imagine how those "good-for-nothings" who were "prone to criminality" used their privileged positions to "enlighten" the population and the Army who were anti-Semitic through and through. In their proclamations, the words "kike" and "Communist" were one and the same. This is how they portrayed the Soviet regime in their artistic posters: A blood-red Devil, with Trotsky's face, rules over an enslaved Russia, which is drenched in blood.

The Kiev *Osvag* distributed this general dispatch throughout the provinces (in Fastiv, Lubny, Smila, Chernihiv, and elsewhere) on the events of October 14/19: "With their guerilla shootings, the Jewish residents helped the Bogun Bolshevik regiment repel the Volunteer Army and retake part of Kiev... Military organizations from Jewish parties fired with machine guns and rifles, they threw hand grenades, they poured boiling water on the Volunteer Army... As soon as the Red Army took Kiev, they began to plunder and commit pogroms... Because the Jews took part *en masse* in the attack on Kiev, and the role that local Jews played in helping the Reds... a great rage has overtaken the Christian population, which the authorities are having great difficulty in subduing" (general dispatch, press bureau No. 17, dated 6/19 October, posted in many towns).[48] Here they were not simply talking about "Jewish shootings" but about a military uprising against the Volunteer Army. And when was this accusation made? On 6/19 October, which is to say, on the very day when in Kiev itself no one still believed the myth of "Jewish shootings," and when General Bredov, the supreme commander of Kiev at the time, called for "mercy for the defeated enemy."

What the military authority could not do openly it did through the hands of sympathetic friends. We have noted how the regime opened

---

48 There is in the Archives of the Editorial Board on Pogrom Materials a printed copy of this dispatch, which was removed from a wall in Ostior (Chernihiv province). By an oversight of the censor, the dispatch was published in the Kiev Yiddish newspaper, *Di velt* [note by the author].

up the cellars of the *Cheka*. And in *Kievlyanin* Shulgin accused "the Jewish hangmen." Now the Jews would have to "drain their bitter cup of repentance." Day in, day out, *Kievlyanin*, the spiritual guide of the Volunteer Army, spewed its poisonous incitement against the Jews, incessantly repeating its philosophy that Jews are Bolsheviks, that Jews are dangerous to Russia, and that there is only one solution: they should "publicly repent for their sins against Russia and leave Russia for good. If not, things would get worse. In his eyes the pogroms by the Volunteer army were nothing but a "Terror Inquisition." The Russian people were terrorizing the Jews because they had ruined their country, and they were right to do so.

With great talent he describes that terror and "the inhuman screams" during the night-time horrors (see the article cited above). But he does not accuse with the "people with knives" who are doing this, or their spiritual leaders. On the contrary, it is the Jews who should ask forgiveness. Here is how he ends the article: "The Russian people listen to those horrified screams and think to themselves, 'Will they (the Jews) finally understand what it means to ruin a country, what it means to bring about equal rights at any price? Will they repent of their sins, cover their heads with ash, and do penance before the whole world because the children of Israel have wickedly joined in the Bolshevik dance of the Devil?'"

That is how Shulgin sees the pogroms, and he gives "the children of Israel" two alternatives. They can either have pogroms as their penance or the "Terror Inquisition," which is to say a state of permanent pogrom without end.

He repeats this demand again and again: the Jews should "repent," they should "excise with their own hands those Jews who had supported both Revolutions" (*Kievlyanin* No. 38, 22 October/5 November 1919, and others). We have already noted the Cossack torture of hanging people to terrorize them into getting something from them. Now this approach had broadened into a complete campaign, a policy, an entire ideology. This approach had become the ideology of the Volunteer Army, which exalted and crowned its newspaper, *Kievlyanin*, which was circulated at no charge and was distributed throughout the Army.

But Shulgin was not alone. The humble Father of the Orthodox Church, Metropolitan Antony of Kiev, was the same. He himself recounts how he received a Jewish delegation which had come to plead with him about the pogroms: "Representatives of the Jewish community came to ask me to publish a proclamation against pogroms. To which I responded that they should first make their coreligionists quit all Bolshevik institutions" (reported in an interview in *Kievskaya Echo* Nos. 42–47, 28 October/20 November 1919).

All the commanders, garrison chiefs, etc. absorbed from the ideologues of the pogrom, both military and political, that the Jews were at their mercy. "You've suffered for 14 days. But how long have we suffered from you all this time? Get out!" was how Col. Karpov, garrison chief in Boryspil answered a Jewish delegation which had come to give him a "gift" of 30,000 rubles and to implore him to stop a pogrom that had lasted two weeks. In the final analysis the fundamental principle that underlies the theoretical campaign against the Jews can be summarized in the frank words of the "dregs," the simple Cossack who said in Bogodukhov, "The Jews must be butchered." And should you ask him why, he will answer in all innocence, "For kikes, no pretext is necessary."

So we see that there is a link between the military conditions of the Volunteer Army — undisciplined, relying on plunder for upkeep — and its military objective — the war against the Bolsheviks. The "kikes" provided the link. The objective, which would have not been easily achieved even if conditions had been better, was lost sight of. The ideology gave the Army a more reachable enemy: no longer the Red Army in its gray uniform, but the Jew in his gabardine. And it gave the Army "permission to go wild for three days." Pogroms against Jews were the ideal solution, they were part of the war against the Bolsheviks. Furthermore, there was a guarantee that Russians, "our own," would not be harmed, and would be happy to let themselves "be saved" only if they did not have to pay for it. "Our own" could be bought, at least their silence could.

The Volunteer Army and its Program on the Jewish Question

Things have their own logic, and logic underlying the ideology of the pogroms required them go deeper. A pogrom was a detail, but what was needed was a general rule, a system that would include the whole issue of the Jewish question. Because it was evident: if Jews were citizens with equal rights, then pogroms would not have been permitted. Pogroms against Jews implied that laws did not apply to Jews. They would not be possible if Jews had equal rights, which would mean that they were "protected by law" like everyone else. This obstacle had to be swept out of the way.

Only one could be true: either equal rights or pogroms. The Volunteer Army had only one answer. We have already noted how Shulgin, in his article on "Terror Inquisition" links Bolshevism, equal rights, and pogroms. As Shulgin sees it, Bolshevism (in his opinion) means "ruining the country," and is a Jewish plot to get their rights. Bolshevism permits Jews to get equal rights at any price. Pogroms, on the contrary, are Russia's way to protect itself. That is why Russia wants to avoid the fate of equal rights for Jews. This leads to the conclusion that the only way to exalt Russia again is by preventing equal rights for Jews.

Shulgin explores this idea in many articles. "There are," he says, "decent Jews and evil Jews... Evil Jews are those who get involved in politics. Jews have shown that in politics they can only wreak devastating ruin, no more. We ask decent Jews to convince their sons and their brothers not to meddle in politics in Russia" (*Kievlyanin* No. 63, 21 November/4 December 1919).

We hear the same from Shulgin's pupil, the infamous Savenko, and others. It is noteworthy that Shulgin does not believe that "decent Jews" will be wise enough to follow his advice. That is why he offers the regime a ready-made program to bring the Jews to their senses: "Jews must be forced out of every position where they might harm the Russian government, which is being reborn. There should be no Jewish officers, officials, or judges. There should be no Jews on city councils, and none in the *zemstovs*,[49] and no mayors (*Kievlyanin* No. 41, 25 October/7 November 1919). Not surprisingly it did not take long for the regime to carry out its leader's program. It was done exactly as Shulgin advised.

And in some cases it had even started before he made his suggestions. They began with Jewish officers, who were summarily expelled. When there were mobilizations, Jews were rejected. Those were the orders of the high command, General Mai-Mayevsky and others. In the petition that a Jewish delegation gave to General Denikin (at a meeting on 26

---

49   Russian: rural councils.

July/8 August 1919) we discover an interesting fact: "In Kharkiv there was a military unit of the Volunteer Army, half of whom were Jews. That unit was sent to fight with a mixed battalion near Zolochev, and fought well in the operation. But the very same day they pulled the Jews out of the battalion and sent them home until the next mobilization." When the delegation pointed this out to General Denikin, he replied: "I warned General Mai-Mayevsky about this, but I knew that he couldn't do anything else. I finally ordered that the Jewish officers be dismissed and held in reserve." The reason was that the Army would not tolerate Jews. For General Denikin and the other generals this should not have prevented them from mobilizing Jewish soldiers. Because we already know from Shulgin's program that danger lay only in Jewish officers — in the rights of Jews — and not in Jewish soldiers, the obligations of Jews.

Then they expelled Jews from city councils. On 4/17 August, for example, Division General Schipner-Markevich gave his first order to the garrison in Cherkasy, which stated: "1. Kuban Cossacks took Cherkasy today, and the city is now part of the territory of unified, indivisible Russia. 2. I order that the city municipal administration assemble, as it was constituted before the Bolshevik overthrow, excluding Bolsheviks and Jews."

General Osovsky did the same in Kremenchug, in his Order No. 1. The only difference here is that he orders not only the expulsion of Jews from the city municipal administration, but also from the City Hall, adding this explanation: "to calm down the population." And the same was done in Niezhyn and elsewhere.

Jews were barred from elections. Jews were crossed off electoral lists for the city hall in Bila-Tserkava and Kiev, following Shulgin's program. This happened to the Jew Ladizhensky, a member of the Kiev city administration. The Governor of the province, Cherniavsky, was given the list to certify. Most of them were members of the administration, among them Ladizhensky (an engineer experienced in city management). The Governor did not want to certify Ladizhensky, and the other candidates, Christians, would not give in.

A compromise was reached over this conflict: Ladizhensky would pretend that he was sick, and therefore unable to serve in the administration. A short time later Ladizhensky was permitted to serve.

The city council wrote up the protocol and presented it to Cherniavsky, who had the right not to certify it within a certain time period. But he did not do so, from which it was concluded that by his inaction he was certifying Ladizhensky in the council. But General Dragomirov intervened unexpectedly, issuing this order: "I hereby remove Ladizhensky from his position as a member of the council" (15/18 October 1919).

This high-level commander, whose assignment it was to supervise all the civilian and military activities in one third of Ukraine, still had the time and sufficient interest to look into small-time Jewish affairs. In one instance four Jewish workers were expelled from the printing office at headquarters because they were Jewish. The central bureau of the professional unions pointed out to the commander that there was absolutely no reason to fire them. To which General Dragomirov responded sharply to the bureau in a rage, warning them that if they ever showed such audacity again, he would bring them before a military tribunal (7/20 November 1919).

And so they put Shulgin's plan into effect. They systematically reduced the Jews to the same status of slaves without rights that they had had in the time of Nikolai. First trample them, then put them in chains. Jews were being degraded even more in the eyes of "the dregs." The lower the Jews fell, the better "the dregs" felt about themselves. The civil rights of citizens did not apply to Jews. Jews were aliens. Especially in light of the atrocities of the Volunteer Army, it didn't take much to see that the laws of common decency did not apply to Jews. The Jews were left on their own. And that kind of abandonment was morally and politically rooted in their lack of civil rights. It was an old story that had been repeated many times in many countries. There was a chain of assumptions and a conclusion: (1) To an army "of low character" and violent "dregs" (2) which maintains itself "in the manner of Wallenstein," that is, from plunder and violence (3) is given the objective of waging war against Bolshevism, that is, the kikes" (the terms "kikes" and Bolsheviks are interchangeable), and these Jews are not protected by the law — and are excluded from civil rights and public life (4) so as to save Russia and the Orthodox Church. (5) Therefore only one conclusion can be drawn: "Murder the Jews and save Russia!"

The Struggle Against Pogroms

Was there no effort at all to stop the pogroms? On paper, why certainly, of course! The military commanders in the towns can show you a mountain of orders that forbid harming peaceful civilians, including Jews. And they rant that anyone who violates the order will be subject to the harshest laws of war and will be shot on the spot. But if you look closely at the actual practice of the war, you will see what that order is really worth. We have already noted that officers (including those of high rank) took part in the pogroms alongside their soldiers and Cossacks. And often it was the officers themselves who started them. Even those officers who did not actually participate with their own hands still shared in the plunder. Not to mention the "contributions" that they extorted. Commanders and garrison chiefs, who were supposed to stop the pogroms, were constantly extorting "contributions" to "uphold order," meaning to issue orders. What more do we need than Sokolov's account about "heavy capital" and a "gigantic train loaded with merchandise and other goods," which he saw in Rostov with "a popular military leader?"

Could the military commanders on the ground really have stopped the pogroms, when they knew that that Army did not take them seriously, and when they themselves participated? There can be no doubt. When you weigh the many orders that were not obeyed, that is evidence, too. The Cossacks got the message. It suffices to consider the case of stopping a pogrom in one town, and the answer becomes quite clear. On 4/17 August 1919, the Volunteer Army took Cherkasy, and it launched a pogrom that very day, which lasted 3 days and took the lives of 150 people and many more who were wounded and raped, not to mention plundered.

The command took note of the pogrom only on 6/19 August, the third day. The commander, centurion Golovk, issued Order no. 3. It mentions pogroms, among other things: "Point 4. I have received many complaints that Cossacks are supposedly plundering, but it turns out that in reality, it is the local people who are plundering. I am furious, and anyone who is caught red-handed will be shot without mercy." This, then, officially absolved the Cossacks and their officers of any responsibility, which is to say the very ones who had perpetrated the pogrom, and they could continue what they were doing without interference. After the third day (the infamous "3 days") the violence subsided, followed by a "quiet pogrom."

Violence and plundering continued. Jewish homes were ransacked, supposedly in the search for weapons. The military command again commented on the pogrom, but now in a patient tone. The new commander in town, lieutenant Vasilyev, issues an order (No. 1, 8/21 August) which states, among other things: "Point 4. Searching houses at will (without an order) are strictly forbidden. Whoever disobeys this order will be treated as a robber. Point 5. I ask you to help the chief of the city police to stop robbers and other criminals. They (the criminals) should be arrested and brought to me." Clearly that order had no more of an impact than the first two, because the very next day the command again addressed the same issue.

This time it was the garrison chief, Captain Yakovlev, but he does not accuse the criminals, and instead chastises and blames the victims. His order states: "I have already ordered the residents to surrender their weapons, their valuable clothes, and their valuable things. And it should have been done all at the same time… Instead they hid their weapons and their (valuable) things, and because of that we are forced to search the houses (Order no. 2 to the Cherkasy garrison, dated 9/22 August)." After they so obviously whitewashed "those who had done the searches," that is to say those who had committed the pogroms, it was a signal to everyone that they were permitted to do anything they wished. And they did, to such an extent that in a few days the authorities again had to take up the pen.

The new garrison chief, Captain Shimkevich, had to speak severely. His announcement said: "The Volunteer Army has routed the Bolsheviks, those evil plunderers and rapists, and has brought peace and security to all citizens alike, whatever their nationality, but I have heard that in a few parts of the city there have been attacks and robberies… I, the garrison chief of Cherkasy, wish to root out such Bolshevik activities, and I am warning the population that I am taking the most severe measures to protect the personal security and possessions of the citizenry. Those who are caught red-handed will be shot without mercy." (Announcement dated 13/16 August).

These "severe" words and "measures" must have frightened no one, because the "quiet pogrom" did not stop, and a new commander of the guard, Colonel Christoforov, had to start all over. Apparently he could not count on his own authority, because he immediately looked for help from a higher rank, General Slashchev, the supreme commander over the entire region, whose proclamation dealt primarily with the peasant revolts and specifically with Makhno's gangs. Here is what it said: "I have been given the responsibility to allow the people the possibility to live peacefully, and I will do it. I will also take responsibility for violence against peaceful residents... I take full responsibility." (Order no. 19, dated 30 October/12 November 1919)

The General's wrath was of no use either. In any case it was almost all over. The Volunteer Army was starting to retreat along the whole front, and mass plundering and slaughters began again. The same Christoforov had to bring it up again a month later (for the umpteenth time), with the threat to "shoot on the spot." It is clear from his order that mass plunder was occurring again, especially against the Jewish residents, supposedly "by people disguised in the uniform of the Volunteer Army. I am convinced that these plunderers are not actually members of the Army... They are undoubtedly criminals who have put on the uniform in order to incriminate the honorable fighters of the Volunteer Army. Therefore I order... shooting on the spot without mercy." (Order no. 20, dated 27 November/10 December 1919).

Christoforov also promises that he will "publicly report the names of all those who are shot." But no one ever has ever seen such a report. That is not surprising, considering the real purpose of the order: to whitewash those who were really guilty, the Cossacks and their officers, while throwing the blame onto the Bolsheviks, meaning, in the Volunteer Army context, the Jews themselves. We have already noted the use of this approach in Niezhyn (see above) and elsewhere.

Looking at these orders that repeat the same thing, with little variation, in different towns, we cannot avoid concluding that the military command in each place issued those orders with these aims: 1. Whitewash those who were actually guilty, the Army, while besmirching the Bolsheviks 2. Keep up appearances for the sake of the supreme commanders 3. Humor the Jews to obtain "contributions." That was how the local military stopped pogroms. But what were the upper echelons doing? They certainly understood what Shulgin had predicted, that "such an army would not last long." They must have grasped that and they must have understood that pogroms weakened the victimizers no less than the victims. For that reason they had to curb the pogroms, for the sake of the Army itself. The survival of the Army was in danger.

But first we must ascertain whether they knew about them and what they knew. We have already noted that a Jewish delegation informed Denikin about the pogroms on 26 July (August 8). To which Denikin replied: "I know more about these excesses than you."

A bit earlier, on July 20 (2 August), Denikin — as well as his whole regime — had been informed of the pogroms by a resolution of the regional conference of the People's Socialist Party in Rostov-on-Don.

On 13/26 September the Ukrainian committee of the Union for the Regeneration of Russia sent Denikin a detailed report on the pogroms and what needed to be done to stop them, with much documentary material.

On the 3rd of October, three organizations, the National Center, the Union for the Regeneration of Russia, and the Union for the National Unification of Russia (which were the pillars of Denikin's advisory Special Council) sent Denikin an outraged memorandum on the pogroms.

At the end of October Professor Odinets, chairman of the Kiev Committee of the Union for the Regeneration of Russia, himself spoke to Denikin about it. In addition, the other high commanders — generals like Dragomirov, Mai-Mayevsky, Bredov, etc., were well-informed of the pogroms by delegations, memoranda, complaints by private individuals, etc. In short, the highest echelons were perfectly well aware of what was happening.

Strictly speaking, we cannot say that they did nothing at all about it. They issued orders forbidding pogroms. But these official prohibitions had absolutely no effect. Worse, they were mocked. In Kiev, for example, there was an assistant police commissioner named Skorokhod in Podol who, it appears, took seriously Bredov's order of 5/18 October (mentioned above). Here is his account of this strange story of what occurred: On 5/18 October he caught criminals (four armed soldiers) red-handed as they were attacking Eliezer Moshinsky's home at Vekhny-Val No. 23. He managed to arrest three of them with eyewitnesses. But he could not investigate the matter further, because disturbing news came that "high superiors" of their military detachment were on their way to help out their pals who had been arrested. So Skorokhod turned over the three men with their stolen goods to the commandant. He soon learned that the men had been released immediately. Skorokhod complained that in such situations the local guard (the police) was totally incapable of stopping armed attacks by military units, which were occurring on a massive scale. He ends his report this way: "The sub-commandant told me secretly, as a friendly warning, that it would go badly for policemen who tried to arrest soldiers, and he counseled me not to do it again. (Report of the assistant police commissioner dated 6/19 October).[50]

And that was how it went in Kiev right in front of General Bredov's eyes. What, then, could we expect of the provinces, where the commanders, the garrison chiefs, etc., often led the pogroms themselves, or at best shared the plunder with the Cossacks? There they didn't merely intimidate the police; they punished them. For example in Pryluk the police arrested four soldiers in the pogrom. The commander of the Semyonov regiment came, gave the police chief a good slapping, and released the soldiers along with their plunder. Is it any surprise that the "struggle" against the pogroms had absolutely no effect?

Much would have been required for that effort to have been successful, especially considering the way the Volunteer Army supplied itself. Above all, the highest commanders needed to have really been sincere and serious about it. The Cossacks and the officers needed to have been convinced that the military leaders fundamentally considered pogroms to be shameful, totally intolerable, and in no way part of their mission and purpose. But for the military leaders to really have been serious, they would have had to — at the very least — considered Jews as citizens with equal rights. They would have to think of Jews as an integral part of the population; who were no worse than others; who could just as well have Bolsheviks among them (since the Volunteer Army considered Bolsheviks to be criminals); and who bore no collective guilt for the actions of the Bolshevik Army.

But could the highest commanders think of Jews that way? Not at all! Because they were the very same Tsarist generals who were steeped in the hatred of Jews and who rejected them as equal citizens. For four

---

50   A similar report was received from Chuvenko, police commissioner in Region Two of Bila-Tserkava [note by the author].

years, during the World War, they had continuously accused the Jews as traitors and spies. It was on their orders that hundreds of Jews had been falsely charged with espionage, as in the trial of Hershonovich in Mariiampil, and in the slander of Jews in the village of Kuzhi (Kovno province), etc. It was on their orders that hundreds of thousands of Jews were banished from the area of the front line — and given 24 hours to leave — with a cruelty such as they never showed towards the citizens of the enemy, during the expulsion from Kovno and Suvalka provinces on 5 May 1915. We have seen that their treatment of the Jews had not changed.

Even their way of making Jews "respectable" remained the same: At the start of the World War the Tsarist generals had seized Jewish hostages in Poland and Lithuania, and now they did the same in Ukraine under Denikin's flag, in Valk on June 18–19 (July 1–2), 1919. Then they methodically fired all the Jews from government and social jobs. They set up a regime in which Jews had no civil rights and were denigrated. They expelled Jewish officers from their Army, as well as doctors (as in Kiev). They expelled Jews from the city governments, even from committees on wartime industrial production. They fired Jewish workers from all government enterprises. It was the highest echelons, the leaders at the top, who did all that. What impression, then, would that have made on the regular officers and Cossacks, especially since it was in their own personal interest that Jews be equated with "Bolsheviks" and "the enemies of Russia." Did the soldier-criminals in Kiev, for example, really believe that General Bredov was serious with his order of 5/18 October against pogroms, when in that very order he made it clear that the Jews were "the defeated enemy," and they should be treated "with mercy?"

The most essential element was missing: sincerity! The attitude of the soldier-criminals towards the Jews was the same as that of those who should have stopped them. The generals, who are generally poor diplomats, could not even disguise the real reason for their sham campaign against pogroms which was: "What will the world say? What will foreign countries say? We have the Entente on our side, which sends us weapons and finances us, and watches over our relations with countries on our borders, in a very complicated international situation. What will they say about our pogroms?"

That was the overriding concern of many generals, Shkuro, Bredov, etc., when they spoke against pogroms. The dictatorship — Denikin himself — saw it that way too. The Jewish delegation of 26 July/8 August pleaded with him to issue a public proclamation against pogroms, and about the Jewish question in general and cited Admiral Kolchak's proclamation in Siberia. To which he replied: "There are Americans there (in Siberia)! I will make a proclamation for all the rest." What will our friends say? — that was the main issue for the generals, who, since it was a military dictatorship, also had to practice diplomacy. They had to welcome an English general, Briggs, and an American general, Jadwin (from the Morgenthau Commission),[51] and they might have to give them an accounting, too. We have already seen from K. N. Sokolov that liberal declarations were staged "for export."

The Cossacks and their officers understood very clearly the underlying spirit of their leaders' "strict orders," so they paid no attention and just did as they wished. Let their "superiors" deal with their "friends" as best they could. One method could always be counted on: convince the "friends" that all Jews were Bolsheviks. That was why *Osvag* was needed, to peddle stories about "Jewish shooting in Novy-Mglyn, Kiev, etc.; about Jewish commissars (when needed, they could turn the Jewish "bourgeois" into commissars, as in Yuzovka; and about Red Legions of Jews (who were nowhere to be found with guns in their hands, to show the "friends"). Their "friends" believed them, or pretended to...

And since the struggle against pogroms was fundamentally lacking in sincerity, the reaction to those who perpetrated them was extremely mild. During the entire period of eight months, we know of only a single case when General Mai-Mayevsky fired another general, Khazov, the commander of the Second Terek Plastun Brigade, because his brigadiers had destroyed Jewish shops in Smila (Order no. 325, dated 11/24 August). That was the official reason. But it is obvious that General Mai-Mayekovsky did not greatly lament the Brigade's atrocities, because they had already previously devastated Cherkasy, and in Smila they dishonored themselves even worse, with murders and the mass rape of Jewish women. Mai-Mayevsky's mild punishment did not in the

---

51 Brigadier General Edgar Jadwin, member of the Henry Morgenthau Commission, sent by the United States to research the situation in Poland from July to September 1919. Its report was published in the *New York Times*.

least deter their pogrom activities. They went on to destroy the Jewish communities in Korsun and Bila-Tserkava, and they perpetrated the wholesale slaughter in Fastiv, with Commander Belogortsev in the lead, which was the worst of the pogroms of the Volunteer Army. In the course of three days they butchered and burned 600 Jews, and burned down the vast majority of Jewish homes and shops, on 9/22–12/15 September 1919.

There was also a case where General Dragomirov put some officers on trial who had the nerve to be plundering after the "three legal days" of pogrom in Kiev on 17/20 October. There was another case — more of a comedy — of a trial of soldier-criminals in Tomashpil. In September 1919 Tomashpil was overrun by the Second Kuban Labinsk Cavalry Regiment, which launched a pogrom lasting five days straight. A delegation of two Christians traveled to Vafniarka, which was the nearest train station, and complained to General Rozenshild von Paulin. The general sent a field court to Tomashpil. When they arrived, the commander of the Labinsk Regiment summoned some Jews, and ordered them to write a letter attesting that his regiment had done no wrong to the Jews.

The head of the field court himself privately advised them not to accuse the Volunteer Army harshly, and in general to be very cautious about their testimony. On the day that the Jews were going to testify before the court, the Cossacks started shooting in the streets, and screaming, "Kikes, go home! Or we'll murder you!" Most of the witnesses and victims ran away. Only a small group of 15–20 people came to the trial. After the trial, the chairman privately told the Jews that some Cossack criminals had been sentenced to death. But the executions would be carried out in Vafniarka, not in Tomashpil, because it would make the regiment look bad.

Whether there had actually been such a sentence, and whether the sentence had been carried out, could not be officially confirmed. But the residents of Tomashpil *were* able to witness this scene: The court wanted to inspect the Cossack wagons, which were overflowing with goods that had been plundered from the Jews. With the very first wagon, the Cossacks began shooting from the courtyards and the streets nearby. The court ran away, and was not seen again near the wagons. Later, when the Labinsk Regiment retreated before the Bolsheviks, they got even with the Jews on 20–21 February (4–5 March) and perpetrated a pogrom in which they murdered many people.

But those were rare, unusual cases. As a rule the soldier-criminals never had to deal with accusations or face any punishment. K. N. Sokolov confirms this when he mentions "the open plundering at the front." He says, "The knowledge that there would be no punishment, turned loose human beings — often decent, peaceful — whom months of bloody warfare had turned into wild beasts." We gradually struggled against this evil. Once in a while plunderers in military uniform were sentenced to death. But those were very rare exceptions. As a rule they plundered the residents systematically without interference. Soldiers of every rank and position did it (p. 193). Sokolov hides the fact that "the residents" in towns and villages were almost always Jews. As a rule the struggle against pogroms consisted only of orders, proclamations, and persuasion. But the more these sermons against pogroms were issued, the less impact they had on the very people who were supposed to learn their lesson. They were practical people, not political, and experience had taught them that though the orders might seem severe, the commanders were mild, and you could count on them!

There were those who thought that an order from General Denikin, the dictator himself, would help. A Jewish delegation asked him to do it on 26 July (8 August). Similarly the Union for the Regeneration of Russia sent Denikin a memorandum on the pogroms on 13/26 September. So did three organizations (the Union for the Regeneration of Russia, the National Center, and the Union for the National Unification of Russia) in their desperate memorandum of 3 October. General Denikin hesitated for a long time, and finally on 25 September (8 October) he issued an order only to the military commander of the Kiev region: "I have had news that the Army is committing acts of violence against Jews. I order that energetic measures be taken to stop such acts. The guilty shall be punished harshly" (published in Kiev newspapers). "I have had news" — thus said General Denikin *two months* after he had been told of pogroms by the Jewish delegation and after he himself had told that delegation, "I know more about these excesses than you."

How far down the Army did Denikin's three sentences reach? And how much of an effect did they have? The clearest answer to that question lies in the continuing pogroms that did not stop for a single day, and especially the pogrom of 17/20 October in Kiev itself (which until then had been peaceful), which was perpetrated right in front of the highest military and civilian authorities. The Union for the National Unification of Russia independently, and also together with the other two organizations, let Denikin know that pogroms were "a terrible blow to our cause before the world opinion of the Allied countries," which was an approach that should have been effective. They pointed out that in addition to his order, it was also necessary 1) to appoint a high-level investigative commission and 2) bring the criminals to justice.

Could the dictator Denikin have carried out such a campaign against pogroms if he had even wanted to? Denikin gave the answer to that question in another context, when he met with the Jewish delegation on 26 July (August 8). They had told him that he had wrought "a miracle" by creating such an army, and asked him to issue an order against pogroms. It would surely be obeyed. To which Denikin replied, "Thank God that they obey my battle commands. But it is not possible to expect more under the present circumstances and the morale of the Army." Clearly the dictator knew his Army better than his officers. Having unleashed "the dregs," "the wild beast," nothing he did would be effective now. And the more that "dregs" were "liberating Russia," i.e. the more they "liberated" Jews of the burden of their lives and possessions and human dignity, the less effective he became. The dregs wished to lead, and not be led.

But it must be said that there had been a time when General Denikin understood how serious a situation the bloodbath of pogroms was for the Army itself, a threat to itself. At that time he had shown courage to say it to the Army, and he had found the right words to do it: "Not long ago we were in Oriol. But a series of mistakes has driven us back to Kuban. Now, on the eve of a determined assault, we must be victorious. Let everyone remember that one of the reasons why our front broke down, and our rear fell into indiscipline — was the murders and the plundering... If our commanders do not immediately root out this evil, our new attack will be for naught. I command that the harshest measures be taken, including the death penalty, against all those who commit murder and plunder, and against those who hide them from the higher superiors, which they are not."

But it was too late, after all that had already happened! He gave that command on 23 January 1920 in the village of Tikhoretsk in the death throes of the Volunteer Army. General Denikin had overestimated his chances. The "Plunder Army," as the Volunteer Army was called in Ukraine, was broken and totally undisciplined. But it did manage to take back Rostov again for two days, February 7–8, but it was forced to retreat. At the end of the month its remnants were driven back to the sea.

Whatever one may think of the "measures" against pogroms taken by the high command of the Volunteer Army, there remains one significant detail which cannot be altered or explained away. Petliura's military units also committed pogroms, including those by big and little "Atamans" (officers), and their attempts to stop the pogroms were no better than that of the Volunteers. But there was one anomaly: a single investigative commission in a single town: Zhitomir. The Volunteer Army did not even have that much. Yes, there was an investigation to be sure, not into the pogroms, but into "Jewish shooting," by Senator Gulayev's commission in Kiev. They censored the respectable press. For example, on 23 September (October 6) 1919, Chernovitz, the editor of the Jewish newspaper, *Di velt*[52] was notified that "no articles about pogroms or assaults committed by people in military uniform shall be permitted to be published." And the Volunteer Army itself hid its atrocities from the world, certain that they would remain unnoticed. Who knows what more horrifying things would have come to light?

---

52   Yiddish: The World.

List of Jewish Communities That Were Destroyed

1. Avdeyevka, Yekaterinoslav province
2. Ignatovka, Kiev province
3. Ovukhov, Kiev province
4. Olshanitsa, Kiev province
5. Okhrimova, Kiev province
6. Ostior, Chernihiv province
7. Orlovets, Kiev province
8. Badievka, Podolia province
9. Baturin, Chernihiv province
10. Bobrovytsia, Chernihiv province
11. Bogodukhov, Kharkiv province
12. Bohuslav, Kiev province
13. Borzna, Chernihiv province
14. Boryspil, Poltava province
15. Boyarka, Kiev province
16. Beybusy (a village), Kiev province
17. Bila-Tserkava, Kiev province
18. Belilovka, Kiev province
19. Gogolevo, Chernihiv province
20. Golovenka (a village), Chernihiv province

21. Germanovka, Kiev province
22. Grebionka, Poltava province
23. Dzhurin, Poltava province
24. Dymer, Kiev province
25. Dremalovka, Chernihiv province
26. Hostomel, Kiev province
27. Horodyshche, Kiev province
28. Valk, Kharkiv province
29. Vasilkov, Kiev province
30. Volchansk, Kharkiv province
31. Verbka, Podolia province
32. Zamekhov, Podolia province
33. Zolotonosh, Kiev province
34. Tagancha, Kiev province
35. Talne, Kiev province
36. Tarashch, Kiev province
37. Tomashpil, Podolia province
38. Tetiiv, Kiev province
39. Trostyanets, Podolia province
40. Triles (Jewish agricultural settlement near Fastiv), Kiev province
41. Tripoli, Kiev province
42. Chervlenska, (a Jewish agricultural settlement near Fastiv), Kiev province
43. Chernihiv
44. Cherkasy, Kiev province
45. Yablonova, Poltava province
46. Yampol, Podolia province
47. Yanovka, Kiev province
48. Yaruha, Podolia province

49. Yenakiev, Yekaterinoslav province

50. Yekaterinoslav

51. Kharkiv

52. Khodorkov, Kiev province

53. Khorol, Poltava province

54. Lozovaya, Yekaterinoslav province

55. Luchinets, Podolia province

56. Makarov, Kiev province

57. Mohilev-Podolsk province

58. Monastyryshche, Kiev province

59. Moshny, Kiev province

60. Miaskova, Podolia province

61. Mykhailivka, Yekaterinoslav province

62. Mezhyrich, Kiev province

63. Novo-Arkhangelsk, Kherson province

64. Novy-Malyn, Chernihiv province

65. Nosivka, Chernihiv province

66. Niezhyn, Chernihiv province

67. Savaran, Podolia province

68. Sviatashin, Kiev province

69. Sinelnikov, Yekaterinoslav province

70. Smila, Kiev province

71. Stavishche, Kiev province

72. Stepanets, Kiev province

73. Pavoloch, Kiev province

74. Pohrebyshche, Kiev province

75. Potoki (a village), Kiev province

76. Poltava, Kiev province

77. Popelna, Kiev province

78. Pushcha-Voditsa, Kiev province

79. Piatigorya, Kiev province

80. Pryluk, Poltava province

81. Fastiv, Kiev province

82. Kaharlik, Kiev province

83. Kalius, Podolia province

84. Kamenskoya, near Yekaterinoslav

85. Kamenka, Kiev province

86. Kobishch, Chernihiv province

87. Kozin, Kiev province

88. Kolibalod, Kherson province

89. Koldubitska (a Jewish agricultural settlement near Fastiv), Kiev province

90. Kaniv, Kiev province

91. Konotop, Chernihiv province

92. Kornin, Kiev province

93. Korsun, Kiev province

94. Kupiansk, Kharkiv province

95. Kurilovtsy, Podolia province

96. Kiev

97. Krivoye-Ozero, Podolia province

98. Kremenchug, Poltava province

99. Rakitna, Kiev province

100. Rozhev (an agricultural settlement), Kiev province

101. Rossovo, Kiev province

102. Ryzhanovka, Kiev province

103. Rikun (a Jewish agricultural settlement), Kiev province

104. Shargorod, Podolia province

105. Shibenoya (a village), Kiev province

Sources

This book is based on the documents in the Archives of the Editorial Board for the Collection and Investigation of Materials Concerning the Pogroms in Ukraine, and in general these materials fall into two categories:

I. The Board's own documents:

1. Special investigations that the Board itself sponsored by sending people to certain locations. Although Kiev was cut off from the rest of the province, and it was dangerous to travel on the trains, especially for Jews, the Board managed to investigate Boyarka, Fastiv, and to some extent the Jewish agricultural community of Koldubitsk-Obraztsova, near Fastiv.

2. Eyewitness testimony from observers and victims. This comprised the bulk of the documentation. We interviewed people on site and homeless people who had fled to Kiev. We used a certain format and were careful in choosing subjects. The testimony was recorded using the person's own words. We tried to interview as many people as possible from the same location, people from different classes, so that there would be an impartial verification of the testimony.

3. Reports from the Board's own correspondents.

4. Official reports (in copies) from government officials.

5. Complaints and appeals by victims to the regime.

6. Documents: proclamations, commands, orders, etc. from the regime, social organizations, etc.

7. Lists of the names of those who had been murdered.

8. Newspaper materials.

II. Documentation from other organizations and institutions that the Board has in its archives (mostly copies). The most important among these are materials are:

A. From the Russian Red Cross (specifically the Relief Committee for Victims of Pogroms of the Russian Red Cross in Kiev). The Red Cross worked on behalf of pogrom victims, sent people to pogrom areas, kept correspondents there, and had an information office in Kiev to collect documentation. The most significant among those materials were:

> 1. Reports from those fully-authorized to do relief work on site. The Red Cross also had: 2. Testimonies of victims and witnesses, 3. Documents, 4. Lists of those who had been murdered.

B. Reports from the Central Jewish Committee for the Assistance of Pogroms (in Kiev), especially the Committee's Legal Office. This office gathered very important documents, especially the Kiev pogrom (eyewitness testimony). There were also:

> 1. Reports from fully-authorized local committees and correspondents, 2. Testimonies of victims, 3. Documents, 4. Complaints and petitions by victims to the authorities, 5. Memoranda from the Committee itself to the authorities and other institutions.

C. Reports from Jewish communities

    a. Kharkiv, especially pogroms in Kharkiv province and massacres on the railroads.

        1. Testimonies of victims.

        2. Hostages in Valk.

        3. The discussion between the Jewish delegation and General Denikin of 26 July (8 August) 1919, and the memorandum that the delegation delivered to Denikin.

    b. Kiev

        1. Testimonies of victims.

        2. Various memoranda.

    c. From the League to Combat Anti-Semitism (Kiev). These are mostly reports to the Prosecutor in the Court concerning plundering and massacres against Jews in Kiev.

    d. From various organizations

        1. From the Union for the Regeneration of Russia (copies of memoranda to General Denikin and General Bredov, with detailed information on the pogroms.

        2. From the organization Poalei-Zion (reports, testimonies).

        3. Various others.

    On the worst pogroms, the Editorial Board and other institutions independently gathered parallel materials, on their own. On those pogroms there are reports both from correspondents and eyewitnesses.

Index

This book need not end here...

Share

All our books—including the one you have just read—are free to access online so that students, researchers and members of the public who can't afford a printed edition will have access to the same ideas. This title will be accessed online by hundreds of readers each month across the globe: why not share the link so that someone you know is one of them?

This book and additional content is available at:
https://doi.org/10.11647/OBP.0176

Customise

Personalise your copy of this book or design new books using OBP and third-party material. Take chapters or whole books from our published list and make a special edition, a new anthology or an illuminating coursepack. Each customised edition will be produced as a paperback and a downloadable PDF. Find out more at:
https://www.openbookpublishers.com/section/59/1

Like Open Book Publishers

Follow @OpenBookPublish

Read more at the Open Book Publishers BLOG

You may also be interested in:

Brownshirt Princess
A Study of the 'Nazi Conscience'
Lionel Gossman

https://doi.org/10.11647/OBP.0003

The End and the Beginning
The Book of My Life
*Hermynia Zur Mühlen. Translation, Introduction
and Comments by Lionel Gossman.*

https://doi.org/10.11647/OBP.0010

The Sword of Judith
Judith Studies Across the Disciplines
*Kevin R. Brine, Elena Ciletti
and Henrike Lähnemann (eds.)*

https://doi.org/10.11647/OBP.0009

Printed in the USA
CPSIA information can be obtained
at www.ICGtesting.com
LVHW020007061123
763136LV00013B/1028

9 781783 74